Fast Bikes

igloobooks

Published in 2014
by Igloo Books Ltd
Cottage Farm
Sywell
NN6 0BJ
www.igloobooks.com

Copyright © 2014 Igloo Books Ltd

Written by Stephen Icke

SHE001 0714
2 4 6 8 10 9 7 5 3 1
ISBN 978-1-78343-540-1

Printed and manufactured in China

CONTENTS

FAST BIKES

Bikes. Fast bikes. The thrill of hearing them, seeing them and riding them. It's the adrenaline rush extraordinaire! You can always spot a biker in the street. They will stop and look around, curiously seeking out a noise they have heard in the distance – an exhaust note, from something fast. It may be the husky, throaty sound from a Ducati or the higher pitched tone of a Yamaha R1. Whatever it is, the sound brings a smile to the face and the sight of the bike may result in a courteous nod to the rider. A nod of acknowledgment, a nod of appreciation.

The competition to create the fastest production motorcycle began in 1894–1897, when Hildebrand & Wolfmüller produced the world's first production motorcycle. It had a 1500cc engine and was capable of 25–28 mph (11–13 kph). The competition ended more than one century later with the production of the 1999–2000 Suzuki Hayabusa. A gentlemen's agreement was then reached among the major motorcycle manufacturers to limit the speed of their production machines to 186 mph (300 kph). This began with some models in the year 2000, and became widespread by 2001.

Many great names have held the prestigious title of "fastest production bike". The Brough Superior, Vincent with the Black Shadow, BSA's Rocket 3 and Triumph Trident are a few famous British examples. Japanese, Italian and German manufacturers have also all produced incredible bikes that push the limits of speed. Yamaha, Ducati, Honda, BMW and MV Agusta are just a few of the stunning, lightning-quick vehicles that have hit the roads.

Whatever machine a bike-lover prefers, they all love to hear, see and ride fast bikes. Quite simply, fast bikes make the hairs on the back of the neck stand up... and long may it continue!

FAST BIKES
150-160 MPH

DUCATI MONSTER

The Ducati Monster first appeared in the Ducati range in the early 1990s when Ducati introduced three Monster models, the M600, M750 and M900. It has been through many reincarnations since then. Over the years, the Monster has had engines from other iconic Ducati bikes such as the 916, the 996 and 998. Whatever the year of manufacture, whatever engine is powering the bike, the Monster has a certain look. It is like a compact bodybuilder, but it is still, unmistakably a Ducati.

In 2001, Ducati introduced the S4, which added the liquid-cooled four-valve superbike engine to the stable. The first Ducati Monster S4 is great fun to ride but full of places for water and dirt to hide. Keeping an S4 looking good and free from corrosion means being dedicated to cleaning it properly. In 2002, a limited edition bike was marketed. This 300 edition S4 Fogarty was named after the racer, Carl Fogarty.

By 2008, the Monster had a large 1078cc engine, a single-sided swinging arm, bigger forks and taller suspension. Known as the Monster 1100 it was based on the successful Monster 696, which sold more than 12,000 models in a single year.

TECHNICAL SPECS

ENGINE	Testastretta L-Twin, 4 Desmodromic valves per cylinder, liquid-cooled
DISPLACEMENT	1198cc
TORQUE	91.8 ft-lbs (125 Nm) @7250 rpm
WHEELBASE	59.5 in (1511 mm)
GEARBOX/DRIVE	6-speed, chain-drive
POWER	145 bhp
TOP SPEED	150 mph (241 kph)

Top: 2013 Monster, displays well in a Milan news conference.

Middle: The oval tail light from the 2013 Monster 1200S model, seen here at the Milan International Motorcycle Exhibition.

Bottom: The Monster 796 using some of its 145 horsepower to pull a wheelie.

The styling of the Monster allows a good view of the 1198cc Testastretta L-Twin engine.

More recently, Ducati introduced the 2014 Monster 1200 S, powered by the four-valve 145 bhp 1198cc Testastretta engine, which took this bike to yet another level.

The riding position is good, so the rider feels stable and in control. With the 1078cc engine beneath you and the slightly stiff suspension (something not unusual on a Ducati), it is possible to make the bike handle easily while taking corners on winding roads. Fitted with wide handle bars and a fairly low-geared, precise gearbox, it has good mid-range power and overall good handling.

This is the sort of bike on which to have fun and it certainly doesn't disappoint. Its ride matches its looks. It has punchy power, it is muscly and almost aggressive, but there is no fuss. Whether the Ducati Monster is parked or on the move, the bike gets the job done. Observers and riders alike all appreciate this masterpiece of Italian engineering.

Showing off its compact muscle at the Thailand International Motor Expo, the Monster always draws a crowd. This bike is a Monster 795.

HONDA VFR 750 RC30

This bike has been around in the UK market since 1990 (introduced in 1987 in Japan), but it is still classed as a quick bike and makes it into the 150–160 mph (240–260 kph) category. It is a classic bike, an icon of its time. It has a distinctive look, with its twin, round headlights and flat, sloping tail fairing. It still turns heads today. Fully faired and painted red, white and blue, this bike looks stunning. Honda looked to the race track for inspiration for this bike, and they found it.

The bike has a V-four, 748cc engine fitted with double overhead camshafts and produces 112 bhp. This engine was based on the earlier RC24 but contains a lot of new parts internally. The clutch, gearbox, crankshaft, connecting rods, pistons and cylinder heads are specific to the RC30. The water and oil pumps are also different, so there is very little similarity between the RC30 and the old RC24. The bike costs twice as much as other 750cc race replicas, but it doesn't matter, this is the bike to have. It was hand-built by the Honda Racing Corporation staff and was virtually the same as the race bike ridden by the racing heroes of the time.

The bike was, and still is, a phenomenon. Steve Hislop, Joey Dunlop and Carl Fogarty all rode one of these bikes at the Isle of Man TT races. The RC30 was replaced by the RC45 in 1993 but with little obvious improvements. It was several years before it had similar success on the track!

For road riders, the RC30 is effectively a race bike, but with additions to make it legal such as lights and mirrors. It is quick. First gear takes you through to 80 mph (129 kph). At the time, no other bike would beat it away from a standing start. With a top speed of almost 150 mph (241 kph) and weighing 408 lb (185 kg), the Honda RC30 has fantastic handling ability and stops well, too. Flexible, light-footed and quick – fantastic!

Rear-end details of the RC30 showing its sleek lines.

TECHNICAL SPECS

ENGINE	liquid-cooled, double overhead camshaft, V-4
DISPLACEMENT	748cc
TORQUE	51 ft-lbs (69 Nm) @7000 rpm
WHEELBASE	56 in (1410 mm)
GEARBOX/DRIVE	6-speed, chain-drive
POWER	112 bhp
TOP SPEED	150 mph (241 kph)

The distinctive twin round headlights and white wheels of the RC30.

The Honda RC30 in all its glory. This bike always draws a crowd with its beautiful styling. Its 748cc engine is capable of 155 mph (249 kph).

The KTM 990 Adventurer, fitted with a
V-twin engine that produces 105 bhp.

KTM 990

The KTM 990 Super Duke model was introduced in 2005. This is a street bike that gets straight to the point. From a company that says it has a passion for speed, this bike does not disappoint. Riding it is not for the faint hearted. To get the best out of the Super Duke riding experience you need to drive it hard. Its angular appearance will certainly draw the eye of passers by.

The twin-cylinder, 999cc engine sounds completely different to the earlier 640 model, which was fitted with a single-cylinder engine. Although the bike looks similar to the 640, it feels different. The 990 delivers great power all the way up from 4000 rpm, right up to the moment it hits the limiter at just under 10,000 rpm. This bike has more than a tendency to lift its front wheel when accelerated hard through the first few gears. When it comes to quality, KTM has a reputation for producing well-engineered bikes and this one is no exception.

Top: KTM twin headlights vertically mounted in a slim fairing.

Middle: Detail of the twin disc stopping power on the front of the bike.

Bottom: Plenty of clearance for off-road fun.

TECHNICAL SPECS

ENGINE	75-degree V-twin with double overhead camshaft
DISPLACEMENT	999cc
TORQUE	73 ft-lbs (99 Nm) @6750 rpm
WHEELBASE	57 in (1450 mm)
GEARBOX/DRIVE	6-speed, chain-drive
POWER	120 bhp
TOP SPEED	151 mph (243 kph)

Another model, the KTM 990 Adventure, also uses the 999cc 75-degree V-twin engine, and produces about 105 bhp. This is slightly lower than the Super Duke, which pushes out 120 bhp. With 120 bhp, the Super Duke achieves speeds in excess of 150 mph (240 kph), which is more than enough on this style of bike. Sitting upright in a headwind of more than 100 mph (160 kph) isn't much fun. Cornering on this bike is a lot more gratifying. By adjusting the suspension, the bike can be made to suit any individual, resulting in enjoyment at every turn.

The KTM 990 is more than capable of tackling roads that are a little more challenging, and is right at home on rough terrain. So, if you are thinking of going somewhere unusual or off the beaten track, this bike is most definitely worth considering. Not only will it deliver, it looks good too, especially in the classic KTM colours of orange and black.

The 990, shown here in the more traditional KTM colours. This bike is capable of 150 mph (241 kph), but the riding style means the rider must hold on tightly.

TRIUMPH DAYTONA 675

A howling engine note, silky smooth handling ability and stunning engine power signal the Daytona 675. This bike is a real winner both on the road or on the track. It is probably the bike that truly put the Hinkley factory, where it was created, on the map. When it was first aired, the Daytona grabbed the attention of the sports bike fraternity.

Although it was launched in 2005 at the NEC International Motorcycle and Scooter show, the bike's development started five years earlier. It is said the Hinkley factory wanted to produce a bike that was true to the old Triumph values. This was their first 'mid-weight' sports bike so they wanted it to be special – and it was. Gorgeous to look at and fantastic to listen to, the bike was a sensational piece of engineering. The Triumph Daytona 675 has a three-cylinder engine, close-ratio gearbox, a claimed 126 bhp and a throaty exhaust note that just makes a biker smile! When it was first released, some bike lovers called it the best British sports bike ever – a true accolade.

TECHNICAL SPECS

ENGINE	liquid-cooled, DOHC, inline 3-cylinder
DISPLACEMENT	675cc
TORQUE	54 ft-lbs (73.2 Nm) @11,700 rpm
WHEELBASE	54.8 in (1392 mm)
GEARBOX/DRIVE	6-speed, close-ratio, chain-drive
POWER	126 bhp
TOP SPEED	156 mph (251 kph)

Top: The Daytona 675 front fairing allowed good aerodynamics.

Middle: The 675, looking good in the Diablo Red livery.

Bottom: This bike is fitted with a relatively short exhaust, but the engine note it produces is sublime.

With a narrow chassis, close-ratio gearbox and stability that allows the bike to corner like a dream, the Daytona 675 guarantees a smiling rider.

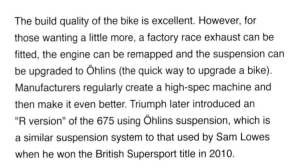

The build quality of the bike is excellent. However, for those wanting a little more, a factory race exhaust can be fitted, the engine can be remapped and the suspension can be upgraded to Öhlins (the quick way to upgrade a bike). Manufacturers regularly create a high-spec machine and then make it even better. Triumph later introduced an "R version" of the 675 using Öhlins suspension, which is a similar suspension system to that used by Sam Lowes when he won the British Supersport title in 2010.

The Daytona 675's three-cylinder engine, narrow chassis and great gearbox allows the rider to focus on the job in hand – the pleasure of fast riding. As for the engineers who set out to produce a sports bike worthy of the Triumph name and in keeping with its values... mission accomplished!

Look what I can do! The 675cc engine, in the right hands, allows the rider to really have some fun.

APRILIA
TUONO FIGHTER

An Aprilia Tuono Fighter, a naked bike first manufactured in 2002, is a machine that is both good cop and bad cop. Its powerful engine and frame come from the Aprilia Mille. For such a big bike, it wheelies with ease. However, once both wheels are on the ground it handles well. The early model's engine was a 998cc 60-degree V-twin that originally delivered 127 bhp. The next generation model will have the latest V-four engine giving out 170 bhp. It's power, power, power all the way from a bike that looks like it means business.

The Tuono Fighter (2003–2008) was fitted with the 998cc engine. This engine was a 60-degree V-twin, four-stroke and liquid-cooled. The bike could achieve speeds of about 160 mph (257 kph) and could travel 0–60 mph (0–97 kph) in just 3.3 seconds. The bike was fitted with carbon fibre parts, gold Öhlin suspension units and Brembo brakes. It certainly had a look about it. Later versions got their power from the engine used in the Aprilia RSV1000R and from a closer ratio gearbox, which increased its power to 133.8 bhp. However, the next generation Tuono will benefit from the longitudinal 65-degree V-four cylinder, four-stroke engine which has a liquid-cooling system, double overhead camshafts and four valves per cylinder. It will also benefit from the Aprilia Quick Shift electronic system in the gearbox. These changes up the stakes considerably.

The Tuono is a fun bike to ride. A steering damper ensures riders don't experience speed wobbles when accelerating hard. Let's face it, when you have a RSV Mille engine in a sit up and beg style machine, you are going to need something to calm it down. The bike corners well and the styling in the later versions has just got better and better. Even the older versions are good bikes to buy and enjoy to the full, especially at the weekend.

The naked bike styling of the Aprilia is eye catching in black and red.

TECHNICAL SPECS

ENGINE	60-degree V-twin, 4-stroke, liquid-cooled
DISPLACEMENT	998cc
TORQUE	86 ft-lbs (117 Nm) @8000 rpm
WHEELBASE	55.7 in (1415 mm)
GEARBOX/DRIVE	6-speed, chain-drive
POWER	133.8 bhp
TOP SPEED	160 mph (258 kph)

Ridden safely on a track, the Tuono can reach the 0-60 mph (0–97 kph) time of 3.3 seconds.

The Aprilia Touno. With its 60 degree V-twin
engine the bike is capable of 159 mph (256 kph).

KAWASAKI GTR1400

A sports tourer capable of eating up the miles at 155–160 mph (249–257 kph). A bike with space to store luggage and take you to your destination in comfort. It rides as though it's not even trying. The GTR1400 has a big 1352cc engine and lots of torque, which makes it a very smooth ride. It has great build quality and feels sturdy beneath you.

The GTR1400 is fitted with the ZZ-R1400 engine but of course had to be detuned to give mid-range power to such a big bike. It is still capable of hitting 160 mph (257 kph) and outputting 152.8 bhp, a big improvement from the 139 bhp produced by earlier models. This is not surprising given that the engine is, after all, a Kawasaki 1352cc, liquid-cooled, four-stroke inline-four. Kawasaki have fitted variable value timing, altering the timing of a valve lift to improve performance, and provide added smoothness.

Even though the GTR1400 is a big bike, the rider can be confident of its reassured cornering ability.

TECHNICAL SPECS

ENGINE	liquid-cooled, 4-stroke inline-four with variable valves
DISPLACEMENT	1352cc
TORQUE	100.5 ft-lbs (136 Nm) @6200 rpm
WHEELBASE	60 in (1520 mm)
GEARBOX/DRIVE	6-speed, shaft-drive
POWER	152.8 bhp
TOP SPEED	160 mph (258 kph)

The GTR1400, in all its glory at the Tokyo Motor Show in 2007.

The grey and blue colour scheme gives this bike the appearance of a machine that is here to do a job. It performs well in the wet or in the dry, with or without the luggage carrying equipment. It is always great to ride. Competition comes in the form of Yamaha's FJR1300 and Honda's Pan European. They have got something to beat with the GTR1400!

The GTR1400 is well appointed. It is definitely a top of the range tourer and weighs 660+ lb (300 kg), but the only time that its weight is apparent is if you over-balance doing a slow U-turn. It is very hard to hold it up once it's going over!

The GTR is a comfortable ride and has a lot of ground clearance when cornering. You might not be a "knee down" sort of rider if you are riding one of the GTR1400 models, but you are still going to be quick. You are also going to be more relaxed on arrival, and have a lot more T-shirts packed in the panniers, therefore smelling a lot nicer at the end of your trip.

With a 1400cc-capacity engine and a top speed of up to 160 mph (258 kph), this bike is a superb tourer.

The super-fast 599cc Yamaha R6.

YAMAHA R6

This supersport bike has been around for more than 15 years but it certainly isn't showing its age. Introduced in the late 1990s, it was the world's first production bike to boast more than 100 bhp (without being modified). The latest machine has an incredible pedigree, developed using race technology. Its eye-popping performance ensures it is still a favourite among supersport riders today.

The bike's high-revving, liquid-cooled, four-stroke, double overhead camshaft, inclined parallel four-cylinder engine runs at 13,000 rpm when delivering its maximum horsepower. Yamaha marketed this bike as the stable mate to the YFF600R. When it was introduced, the race replica bike made the competition stand up and take notice. Nothing else matched the bike until Suzuki introduced the GSXR-R600 (R6) in 2001. There is no doubt this bike was, and still is, pretty special.

By 2003, the R6 was given a fuel injection, and later a delta box design frame enhanced it further. With the development of electronics, the bike was given a Yahama Chip Controlled Throttle (YCC-T) and an engine management system. Yamaha engineers then added a variable length intake system to optimise the bike's power using a Yamaha Chip Controlled Intake (YCC-I).

Top: A winning bike on road or on track.

Middle: The sleek and aerodynamic tail of the R6.

Bottom: British racer Sam Lowes' R6, seen at the Milan International Motorcycle Exhibition in 2013.

TECHNICAL SPECS

ENGINE	liquid-cooled, 4-stroke, double overhead camshaft, forward-inclined parallel 4-cylinder, 16-valve
DISPLACEMENT	599cc
TORQUE	48.5 ft-lbs (66 Nm) @10,500 rpm
WHEELBASE	54.1 in (1375 mm)
GEARBOX/DRIVE	constant mesh, 6-speed, chain-drive
POWER	108 bhp
TOP SPEED	160 mph (258 kph)

The bike now produces more than 130 bhp, ensuring it maintains its top-end performance in today's market. The R6 has an excellent ability to turn, which is its true trademark feature.

For the rider, this bike delivers smoothly. It is also responsive and very quick – easily capable of 160 mph (257 kph). This bike is comfortable and great to ride, and the rider just knows it's going to do what it is asked. With the right pilot in the seat, the bike is capable of giving some of the bigger-engined bikes a run for their money, especially on twisting roads.

With its red and white colour scheme, this 2006
R6 has the looks to match its outstanding top speed.

YAMAHA FZ1

The FZ1 is a naked street bike. Its acceleration throughout its engine range is smooth and although it doesn't have all the fairings of a sports bike, it is no slouch! The bike is capable of hitting about 160 mph (257 kph). In fact, Yamaha class the FZ1 as a sports bike. You can comfortably ride this bike in any city centre and enjoy the performance associated with riding a sports tourer. The bike has a great presence and is considered one of the best sports tourers around.

The FZS1000 (launched in the United States as the FZ1 in 2001) and later known as the FZS1000S, boasted a Yamaha YZF-R1 engine and was originally mounted in a tubular steel frame. Although most of the engine remained unchanged, Yamaha had to make some modifications, introducing a heavier crankshaft and balance shaft. This was to ensure the bike had a less aggressive, more relaxed feel when getting to, and maintaining, cruising speeds.

By 2006, the Yamaha FZ1 had been given a new engine, chassis, suspension and body work. The engine is a 998cc double overhead camshaft, 20-valve tuned R1 engine. It was tuned to improve the mid-range torque. The chassis, a die-cast aluminium diamond-shaped frame, houses the new engine that brought the bike up to date with its rivals. Early Yamaha FZ1 models were prone to what was called "throttle snatch" (which can make riding exciting for all the wrong reasons!), so fuel injection was introduced, which solved the problem.

Road testers say it is hard to fault the FZ1. The bike is effortless when flicked into corners and it handles well when on good tyres. It's an enjoyable bike to ride – comfortable and well equipped, but still incredibly rapid and able to reach speeds of 160 mph (257 kph). This bike sits comfortably alongside its competition from Suzuki in the form of the Bandit and the Honda CBF1000. Reliability problems with the FZ1 Fazer are very rare, making it a great all-round bike.

The FZ1 is a great ride in all weather and road conditions – even snow!

TECHNICAL SPECS

ENGINE	liquid-cooled, 20-valve, DOHC, inline 4-cylinder
DISPLACEMENT	998cc
TORQUE	78 ft-lbs (106 Nm) @8000 rpm
WHEELBASE	57.1 in (1450 mm)
GEARBOX/DRIVE	constant-mesh, 6-speed with multi-plate clutch
POWER	150 bhp
TOP SPEED	160 mph (258 kph)

If you don't want to ride the FZ1 in the snow, at 150 bhp, the bike is just as great a ride on sunny days.

The bike's great inline four-cylinder is shown
off at the Sydney Motorcycle Show in 2006.

The MV Agusta Brutale 1090R with large-diameter twin
front brakes to counteract the power of the 1078cc inline
four-cylinder engine.

Street bike style with
cornering fun included!

MV AGUSTA BRUTALE

This is a fierce street bike that looks the business. It is compact and full of power and character. This bike has seen many developments since its introduction in 2006. Engine sizes have varied from 748cc to 1078cc, and the latter engine is fitted in the Brutale 1090RR. MV Agusta has a long pedigree of producing great bikes. On the race track their bikes have been ridden by some of the most famous and talented riders in history: Mike Hailwood, Phil Reed and Giacomo Agostini. MV Agusta is now owned by Harley Davidson but don't think this bike is anything other than a full Italian muscle bike.

The Brutale model range includes the Brutale 750S, Brutale 910S and R models, Brutale 1078RR, and more recently the 990R and 1090RR.

TECHNICAL SPECS

ENGINE	inline 4-cylinder, 4-stroke, double overhead camshaft and 16 radial valves
DISPLACEMENT	1078cc
TORQUE	83 ft-lbs (113 Nm) @8000 rpm
WHEELBASE	56.6 in (1438 mm)
GEARBOX/DRIVE	6-speed, chain-drive
POWER	142 bhp
TOP SPEED	160 mph (258 kph)

The 1090RR has the 142 bhp inline four-cylinder 1078cc motor, which has same basic layout as the Brutale 1078RR. This bike, however, has the advantage of a dual power map for maximum performance and is fitted with an eight-stage traction control system. It is also lighter than the 1078RR. The 1090RR's engine has a unique double overhead camshaft with four valves per cylinder, which are arranged in a radial pattern. The engine uses two forms of cooling – water and oil – each with a separate radiator. Stopping power is provided by Brembo monobloc front calipers, which give maximum braking efficiency on 12.6 in (320 mm) diameter discs. The rear disc is smaller with a diameter of 8.3 in (210 mm), and has four-piston calipers. The quality of the 1090RR is superb. In fact all Brutale models have proved to be reliable and this one is no exception.

The ergonomics of the early versions were found by some to be cramped and uncomfortable. Later models have a better, more refined riding position. Taking this bike on the road or track feels smooth and easy, with or without a fairing fitted. The Brutale corners with ease and has enormous grip and composure as the throttle feeds in the power. It is a lot of fun.

A Brutale 920 being put through its paces, showing the ease with which it corners.

FAST MOTORBIKES
160-170 MPH

The distinctive look of the V-Max. In black and
chrome, it looks tremendous.

Top: Detailed view of the Yamaha.
The bike can hit 160 mph (258 kph).

Bottom: A great shot of the 1679cc
engine, which produces 174 bhp.

YAMAHA
VMX1200
V-MAX

This beast has been around since 2008. To say it is a little hard to tame is an understatement. Although early models produced only 95 bhp, later versions produced 197 bhp from the V-four engine and were capable of hitting 160 mph (258 kph). However, this bike is not an easy one to ride. It is a handful at the best of times, but it will put a smile on the rider's face as the torque tries to rip your arms from your shoulders!

The Yamaha V-Max was first manufactured in 1985 and immediately made people sit up and take notice. It quickly became known for its distinctive styling and powerful V-four engine and shaft drive. The engine was a double overhead camshaft, liquid-cooled V-four that had previously been used in the Yamaha Venture, but tuned for use in the V-Max. The bike also had 'V-boost'. This was an automatic system that opened/closed butterfly valves in the intake manifold to match the requirements from the throttle.

TECHNICAL SPECS

ENGINE	liquid-cooled, double overhead camshaft, V-4
DISPLACEMENT	1679cc
TORQUE	123 ft-lbs (166.8 Nm) @6500 rpm
WHEELBASE	66.9 in (1700 mm)
GEARBOX/DRIVE	5-speed, slipper clutch, shaft drive
POWER	197 bhp
TOP SPEED	160 mph (258 kph)

As time went by, Yamaha replaced the V-Boost with YCC-I and YCC-T systems (Yamaha Chip Controlled Intake and Throttle systems). This was part of a complete redesign in 2009. Other features included an all-aluminium frame with a 1679cc liquid-cooled, V-four, double overhead camshaft engine used as a stressed member of the chassis, an electroluminescent instrument readout, anti-lock brakes and a slipper clutch. The fuel tank was even put under the seat.

The Yamaha V-Max delivers smooth power up to about 4000 rpm, followed by a step-change to get your attention. Its handling is not the best – the back end feels like it's snaking about when the throttle is applied, but nonetheless, it has a cult following. If you like thrills all the way, this bike will have you laughing, grinning and wanting another ride.

Big engine, big bike, big fun, even with the Yamaha chip control throttle.

The Ninja ZX-6R with centralised weight
distribution means great cornering.

KAWASAKI ZX-6R

The ZX-6R was first introduced in 1995. It looked a lot like the ZX-9R launched a couple of years previously. It also had the Kawasaki ram air intake that had been developed for the ZZ-R1100. Capable of 0–60 mph (0–97 kph) in fewer than 4 seconds and boasting more than 100 bhp, this bike was going to be around for a long time. Through many developments it is now hitting speeds of 160 mph (257 kph).

Since the bike's introduction it has undergone regular updates by the Japanese manufacturer to ensure it keeps its place alongside the competition from Yamaha, Suzuki and Honda. It initially had a 599cc engine, then subsequently a 636cc motor and currently a 599cc powerhouse. In the late 2000s, the bike was made lighter, and given a change of forks and a new under seat exhaust system, which resulted in a smoother ride.

Top: Close up of the ZX-6R nose fairing.

Middle: Lifting the front wheel of the 599cc supersport bike poses no problem.

Bottom: The bike has great grip in the corners, even knee-down.

TECHNICAL SPECS

ENGINE	4-stroke, liquid-cooled, double overhead camshaft, 4-valve cylinder head, transverse inline 4-cylinder
DISPLACEMENT	599cc
TORQUE	46.67 ft-lbs (63.27 Nm) @11,900 rpm
WHEELBASE	54.9 in (1394 mm)
GEARBOX/DRIVE	6-speed with slipper clutch, chain-drive
POWER	115 bhp
TOP SPEED	161 mph (259 kph)

All in all, the developments made to the ZX-6R have meant it has successfully evolved into a bike that maintains some of its original character, but is more forgiving and rider friendly. With the inline four-cylinder engine delivering 115 bhp and speeds of 161 mph (259 kph), the Kawasaki factory have ensured the bike is still fast by modern standards. The manufacturers didn't forget to make it more rideable though. The bike now sports a race-developed steering damper, and as a result of the introduction of changes to the engine mounts, frame and swinging arm, it has greater rigidity. Changing the angle of engine lean and centralising weight has led to a bike that is easier for the rider to turn into the corners without any hassle.

The fabulous 599cc engine, ABS brakes, traction control and all the other transformations made to the ZX-6R mean the bike is more forgiving than it was in the early days, less of an animal. The bike is now more refined but still delivers the excitement of riding a supersport 600 at its best.

On the race track the Kawasaki ZX-R6 looks great as it corners.
The bike is capable of reaching speeds of 160 mph (258 kph).

BMW K1300S

BMW's motorcycle history began in 1921 when they commenced manufacturing engines for other companies. Today, BMW create bikes for all sectors of the market. The K1300S is BMW's ultimate tourer. The bike's only real competition in this sector comes from the Hayabussa and Kawasaki's ZZR1400. The K1300S is an admirable contestant. The bike is not famed for stunning looks but is still quick for its size and can travel 0–60 mph (0–97 kph) in 3.2 seconds.

Although this bike might not stand out in a crowd and is reserved in comparison with the competition's styling, don't be fooled. The K1300S is equipped with a German engineered water-cooled, four-stroke, inline four-cylinder engine that has plenty to offer. It gives thrilling acceleration, smooth power and bags of torque right across the rev range to take you up to 165 mph (266 kph). The BMW K1300S is a bike that has been designed to deal with just about everything. To help it do that the bike can be fitted with an ingenious electronically adjusting suspension, traction control and a whole host of other options, should you so desire.

So, with one of the best large engines around, and renowned BMW quality and reliability this bike will take you anywhere you want to go, and it will do this in comfort and with subtle style. It is heavy at 560 lb (254 kg), but this is compensated for by an engine that is tilted forward to centre the mass. The bike also comes with lots of optional extras, so you can tailor it to your needs. Its shaft drive and a constant mesh six-speed gearbox in conjunction with its big 175 bhp output engine means that come rain or shine this bike is up to the challenge. It meets that challenge at speed and with ease.

Top: A great view of the BMW K1300S touring bike's front, which helps to protect the rider at speeds of 165 mph (266 kph).

Bottom: The K1300S may not be light, but the bike can negotiate corners well.

TECHNICAL SPECS

ENGINE	water-cooled, 4-stroke, inline 4-cylinder engine, 4 valves per cylinder, double overhead camshafts
DISPLACEMENT	1293cc
TORQUE	103 ft-lbs (140 Nm) @8250 rpm
WHEELBASE	62.4 in (1585 mm)
GEARBOX/DRIVE	constant mesh, 6-speed gearbox, shaft drive
POWER	175 bhp
TOP SPEED	165 mph (266 kph)

The BMW K1300S, pictured here, is plain, simple and stylish.

TRIUMPH DAYTONA 955i

The Triumph Daytona 955 is a sport bike manufactured between 1997 and 2006. When originally launched, it was called the Triumph T595 Daytona. At the time, it was thought that the bike had an engine capacity of 595cc, when in fact the engine was 955cc. Although the 955 was quick, it had stiff competition from Yamaha's R1, the Honda Fireblade and the Suzuki GSX R1000, all of which were established as outstanding bikes.

Unfortunately, the Triumph never really hit the same dizzy heights as the R1, Fireblade and GSX R1000. However, the 955 is still a fast superbike that handles well. The three-cylinder engine delivers plenty of low-down drive and top-end grunt. The 955i version of the bike is capable of a top speed of 165 mph (265 kph) and is difficult to find fault with, especially on the roads, which is where most of us ride this bike. Fitted with a 955cc, liquid-cooled, inline three-cylinder, four-stroke engine it pushes out 129 bhp. In later models this increased to 147 bhp, which means it is more than capable of bringing enjoyment to the rider.

TECHNICAL SPECS

ENGINE	liquid-cooled, inline 3-cylinder
DISPLACEMENT	955cc
TORQUE	74 ft-lbs (100 Nm) @8200 rpm
WHEELBASE	56.3 in (1431 mm)
GEARBOX/DRIVE	6-speed, chain-drive
POWER	147 bhp
TOP SPEED	165 mph (266 kph)

Top: Rear wheel detail.

Bottom: With a top speed of 165 mph (266 kph), the 955i corners well, too.

The Daytona 955i may have 147 bhp and an inline
three-cylinder engine, but it looks great on the side stand, too.

Initial problems with earlier models were no longer present in the 955i, and the price of this bike, when new, was considerably lower than the competition. This presented riders with a decision. What to purchase – the more expensive Japanese "top of the class" bike or the cheaper, more comfortable, very capable, British bike. Despite being slightly heavier, the Triumph was better on the roads according to some riders. Just in case riders wanted something a little different, there was even a limited edition model introduced in 2002, the 955i Centennial, which only came in one colour – British Racing Green!

In British Racing Green or any other colour for that matter, the Triumph 955i is great bike to ride on the road. It is stable, reliable and quick.

A triumph of British engineering to rival the Japanese.

A KTM RC8 rider checking the bike can corner with style. Tick.

KTM
1190 RC8

The first generation KTM 1190 RC8 appeared in 2008. The original model had a 1148cc V-twin engine and was the first superbike for the Austrian based manufacturer. The RC8 model was joined by the RC8 R the following year. These were fitted with larger 1195cc engines but it was the styling of the RC8 that made this bike turn heads. It was more than a bit of a divergence from normal styling.

It's not just the RC8's looks that are impressive. From 2009, it contained the 1195cc V-twin engine that is now 'twin spark', which means that each cylinder has two spark plugs per cylinder, only one of which is firing below 7000 rpm. The engine is mounted in a trellis steel frame, with double-sided swinging arm and high spec forks (inverted). When the throttle is opened with enthusiasm, both plugs fire and the bike uses its 170 bhp to propel you along at an impressive 170 mph (274 kph).

Top: A touch of customisation – colour coordinated chain and sprocket.

Middle: A little more customisation in matching orange.

Bottom: Detail of the Öhlin shock absorber fitted to a 2008 RC8.

TECHNICAL SPECS

ENGINE	4-stroke, double overhead camshaft, 75-degree V-twin with twin spark
DISPLACEMENT	1195cc
TORQUE	88 ft-lbs (119 Nm) @8,000 rpm
WHEELBASE	56.1 in (1425 mm)
GEARBOX/DRIVE	6-speed, chain-drive
POWER	170 bhp
TOP SPEED	170 mph (274 kph)

Through its development, the RC8 has lost the original gear
selection and snatchy throttle issues. It is now powerful, usable and
has top tier handling abilities, and can be personalised. Riders can
make lots of individual adjustments to ensure that this bike is their
perfect fit. The adjustments involve not only functions such as brake
levels, but also features such as handle bars and footrest positions.
Once the bike is adjusted perfectly, the RC8 doesn't have to be
ridden hard to give an ultimate performance, unlike other V-twins.
It does like to take corners at speed though. Any rider will gain
enormous pleasure from the unique styling... and the performance.

A lovely view of the rear and 75-degree
V-twin engine. Distinctive RC8 styling.

Cornering, knee-down, the Ducati 1098 feels built for speed.

DUCATI 1098

The Ducati 1098, launched 2007–2009, with classic Ducati styling, has more design elements in common with the older 998 than with its predecessor the 999, especially with the return of horizontal headlights. It boasts a powerful V-twin engine producing 160 bhp, which is capable of delivering a (manufacturer's claimed) top speed of 170 mph (274 kph) and a 0–60 mph (0–97 kph) time of fewer than 3.0 seconds – later variations built on this to achieve 180 mph (290 kph). The iconic 90-degree V-twin Desmodromic engine sounds great through the under-seat exhaust system. The bike however is no easy ride, it demands the rider's complete and undivided attention.

The Ducati 1098 was the Bologna factory's reply to the Suzuki GSXR 1000 and Yamaha's R1. The factory also produced an 'S' version which was capable of 180 mph (290 kph). In the UK demand was so high when it was launched that it sold out and customers had to place orders...and wait!

The Ducati 1098 is the first ever road bike to be fitted with dual, radially-mounted four-piston 13 in (330 mm) Brembo monobloc front brakes. Its stopping performance is tremendous, but its looks alone warrant a purchase.

Top: The classic Ducati red looks great from any angle.

Bottom: Ducati's twin under seat exhaust system which helps to produce its unmistakable sound.

TECHNICAL SPECS

ENGINE	90-degree, V-twin cylinder, 4-valve per cylinder Desmodromic, liquid-cooled
DISPLACEMENT	1099cc
TORQUE	90.4 ft-lbs (123 Nm) @8000 rpm
WHEELBASE	56.3 in (1,430 mm)
GEARBOX/DRIVE	6-speed, chain-drive
POWER	160 bhp
TOP SPEED	180 mph (289 kph)

The Ducati 1098 also boasts some gorgeous bodywork, plus a 1099cc engine. However, its predecessor, the 999 was more user friendly, for example, when increasing mid-corner speed at maximum lean (if the rider is capable of taking it to those sorts of angles…on a track, obviously). The 1098 is different. It responds as soon you touch the throttle, but it's still rideable. The suspension and chassis need to be worked if you want to ride the bike to its full potential.

The 1098 has a different riding position to the 999. The seat height is raised and angled putting more weight on the front of the bike, giving extra leverage when turning the 1098 into corners. Its standard suspension settings front and rear are stiffer than the 999 and the chassis is also more rigid driving through the corners or when changing direction. Get it right as a rider and this is an outstanding bike.

In eye-catching yellow, the 1098 looks
like it just wants to be ridden – hard.

BUELL 1125R

Buell began manufacturing motorbikes in 1983. Started by Erik Buell, a former Harley Davidson engineer, and based in the United States, it is not surprising that some Buell bikes are powered by Harley Davidson engines. By 2003, Buell was a wholly-owned subsidiary of Harley Davidson and by 2009, they had ceased trading. The 1125R was introduced in 2007. It has a 1125cc Helicon V-twin engine made by BRP-Powertrain (Rotax) of Austria. It is liquid-cooled 8-valve double overhead camshaft, four-stroke 72-degree V-twin with six gears and a belt final drive. This bike delivers a power with a kick to it. Using this type of engine makes it very different to the bikes produced by Honda, Yamaha and Ducati.

The 1125R has a top speed of 170 mph (274 kph) from an engine with 146 bhp, and a good reliability record. Early versions are somewhat of a hard ride on bumpy roads and vibration is an issue. No surprise that a year after its introduction, Buell created a heavily upgraded version of the 1125R.

Top: Sleek fairing and slim lights at the front of the bike.

Bottom: The powerhouse. A Rotax Helicon 72 degree V-twin.

TECHNICAL SPECS

ENGINE	Rotax Helicon 72-degree V-twin, liquid-cooled
DISPLACEMENT	1125cc
TORQUE	82 ft-lbs (111 N. `
WHEELBASE	51.1 in (1375 mm)
GEARBOX/DRIVE	6-speed, belt-final drive
POWER	146 bhp
TOP SPEED	170 mph (274 kph)

The Buell looking good in all-black trim.

The bike isn't exactly slow over a standing 0.25 mile (0.4 km), taking a little under 10.5 seconds, but it certainly isn't a high revving beast, hitting the red line at just over 10,000 rpm. However, it was a bike in which Erik Buell had faith. So in 2009, Erik Buell Racing was established. This independent company developed and used race versions of the 1125R model.

Although it may have been seen as a bit of an oddity, this bike deserves its inclusion. Why? It is an American superbike not just because it is capable of reaching 170 mph (274 kph), but also because it was and still is different. Different to the other superbikes from Italy, Japan and the UK. Different is good.

This bike is happy on smaller roads as well as having straight line speed.

FAST MOTORBIKES
170-180 MPH

APRILIA RSV1000

The establishment of Aprilia's RSV1000 was made in 1998 with the RSV1000 Mille. The bike was 100 per cent a sports bike. Blisteringly quick, happy being thrown into corners, manoeuvrable and, importantly on a bike like this, the brakes were first rate. Driven by a 998cc, 60-degree V-twin, it originally reached 165 mph (266 kph). The Mille was updated a couple of times with major changes to its power, gearbox and bodywork. In 2004, the Italian company introduced the awesome RSV1000R and even a tricked-up version, the RSV1000R Factory.

There is no doubt that the Mille is good despite some electrical issues as the bikes age. RSV1000's are tricky around town, and with stiff suspension bumpy roads weren't that much fun either. All of that pales into insignificance as the RSV1000R arrived in 2004. Why? This bike is most definitely not for the fainthearted. This is a high performance bike without a doubt. It's a big Italian twin, so no surprise that as a rider you must show it who is in charge. It has copious amounts of bottom-end torque, a beefy mid-range and adrenaline-inducing top speed. With 143 bhp and a top speed of 172 mph (277 kph), the bike can be a bit of a challenge on the road especially. Speeds above the UK legal limit is where this bike is more than comfortable.

Top: RSV1000's fairing would not look out of place in a Sci-Fi movie!

Bottom: Rear detail of the Aprilia.

TECHNICAL SPECS

ENGINE	liquid-cooled, V-twin
DISPLACEMENT	998cc
TORQUE	76 ft-lbs (103 Nm) @8000 rpm
WHEELBASE	55.7 in (1415 mm)
GEARBOX/DRIVE	6-speed, chain-drive
POWER	143 bhp
TOP SPEED	172 mph (277 kph)

The RSV showing its style and ability when on track. On the road, the twin headlights make the bike visible to other road users.

The RSV 1000R Factory has some extra kit, such as a fully adjustable Öhlins Racing rear monoshock, adjustable Öhlins steering damper, forged aluminium wheels and various carbon fibre parts.

If you are an Italian V-twin fan then you cannot ignore this bike. As you would expect, it is gorgeous to look at and has that V-twin sound. So what if it is challenging to ride? It's going to give hours of enjoyment and excitement. Although you can acquire a bike with similar credentials from a Japanese factory, it won't be the same!

Italian styling at its best. The subtle but stunning colour scheme of the RSV1000 looks magnificent.

SUZUKI GSXR 750

The Suzuki GSX-R750 is a 750cc capacity bike, introduced in 1985. It was one of the first of the modern race-replicas developed for use on the road but using race bike technology. Development continues on the bike known as the Gixer. It still only has the bare essentials, but why add weight? This bike has always been about speed. Modern versions recording speeds of 175 mph (282 kph).

The original model featured a lightweight aluminum alloy frame, and an oil-cooled engine. Why? To save weight. The water-cooled engines at the time were heavier and Suzuki wanted to minimise rather than increase weight.

Top: Front end detail from an early GSX-R750.

Middle: Well-engineered with a quality finish – everywhere.

Bottom: A digital read-out fitted to a customised GSX-R750.

TECHNICAL SPECS

ENGINE	liquid-cooled, 16-valve, 750cc inline-four
DISPLACEMENT	750cc
TORQUE	86.3 ft-lbs (117 Nm) @11,200 rpm
WHEELBASE	54.7 in (1390 mm)
GEARBOX/DRIVE	6-speed, chain-drive
POWER	148 bhp
TOP SPEED	175 mph (282 kph)

The Gixer in all its glory with the traditional Suzuki colour scheme.

To celebrate the 20th anniversary of the GSX R750, Suzuki launched an anniversary model, which included custom paint, custom exhaust, a blue seat and even a blue chain, and of course 20th anniversary decals. By 2007, the bike had a new compact and lightweight four-stroke, four-cylinder, liquid-cooled engine designed for overall weight reduction, increased combustion efficiency and power delivery. It also had a re-designed cylinder head with a compact combustion chamber, higher compression ratio, more aggressive camshafts lifting titanium valves. Alongside all the technical changes, riders can also adjust the suspension and footpegs to enable them to get the bike set up perfectly to their unique requirements.

The Gixer is insatiable when it comes to revs – the bike is always hungry for more. It accelerates like a rocket and achieves a stunning top speed. This bike will take you 0.25 mile (0.4 km), from a standing start, in under 11.3 seconds. Throughout the years the engine has always had a reputation of being bulletproof. So, stepping astride this incredible motorcycle means the rider is in for an impressive ride every single time.

A versatile bike, seen here racing in the Pikes Peak International Hill Climb in Colorado, United States.

Main: Pushing the DB8 to the limit.

BIMOTA DB8

The 'D' in DB8 indicates that this bike has a Ducati engine, and the '8' means that it is the eighth bike in the series. Other Bimota models used engines from Honda, Suzuki, Kawasaki and Yamaha and these all had different model numbers, for example, "S" models used Kawasaki engines. The powerhouse in the DB8 is the Ducati 1198cc, 170 bhp engine. It is the successor to the DB7 which used the Ducati 1098cc engine. Bimota has married a great engine with an in-house designed chassis resulting in an exotic bike.

As the bike weighs less than 420 lb (190 kg) it just keeps on pulling when the throttle is opened. The power from the 90-degree V-twin engine is delivered smoothly until it hits its top speed of 180 mph (290 kph). It's a genuine, unadulterated superbike. The frame, suspension, electronics and the engine all work in superb harmony to give the rider exactly what they are looking for from a superbike. The configuration of the bike is more accommodating for taller riders as this model has a twin seat arrangement.

Top: The simple-but-effective swinging arm.

Middle: Lightweight front discs.

Bottom: Weight reduction seen clearly here on the clutch lever.

TECHNICAL SPECS

ENGINE	Ducati 90-degree twin, liquid-cooled, Desmodromic 4-valve
DISPLACEMENT	1198cc
TORQUE	99 ft-lbs (134 Nm) @8000 rpm
WHEELBASE	56.3 in (1430 mm)
GEARBOX/DRIVE	6-speed, chain-drive
POWER	170 bhp
TOP SPEED	180 mph (290 kph)

Bimota's history has been a little rocky. In the late 1980s they had some success in the World Superbike championships, but a series of events in the late 1990s forced Bimota to file for bankruptcy and close. Luckily for the motorbiking fraternity, in 2003 a group of investors purchased the rights to the Bimota name and designs and restarted the company. Since then they have produced some fantastic bikes, not least the DB8. A bike some riders say has better handling than the Ducati, which is powered by the same 1198cc, 90-degree twin, liquid-cooled, desmodromic four-valve engine.

One of the distinctive features about this bike is the naked appearance of the rear end. Fairings end earlier than on other bikes, meaning that you can see more of the engine and swinging arm. This bike is quick, it has slightly unusual looks, but most of all it is beautiful and very capable of doing the business.

This DB8 rider is wearing smiley knee pads, and you can bet there is a smile on his face, too!

APRILIA RSV 4

The RSV4 is Aprilia's flagship model. The factory also offer two other bike models: the RSV4 Factory and RSV4 R. Production of the RSV4 began in 2008 and the motorcycle was unveiled in Milan, Italy in the same year. It is powered by a V-four, 65-degree 999.6cc engine, which was the company's first production four-cylinder engine. Aprilia claims it was designed for superbike racing and that the engine will produce more than 200 bhp. Aprilia raced the RSV4 in the 2009 Superbike World Championship season and won the championship with Max Biaggi in 2010 and 2012.

The RSV4 R is an incredibly well-balanced, fine-handling sports bike. It is one heck of a bike, hitting high speeds and packing a punch at 181 bhp. Since its introduction, Aprilia have added more technology to the road bikes, especially on the RSV4 Factory model. The rider benefits from race technology such as ABS, traction control with eight different settings, wheelie control with three settings, launch control (for track use) and a quick shift system for rapid gear changes. The RSV 4R has basically the same as the RSV 4 Factory but with less electronic wizardry and a lower spec frame. The Factory model is also fitted with Öhlins suspension and is slightly leaner and meaner. On the RSV 4R the Showa forks and Sachs rear shock ensure a bucketful of confidence for the rider.

Top: The powerhouse in the frame. Compact, neat, integral.

Bottom: Black livery. RSV4 on the fairing. Two large diameter discs. Subtle, but you know its going to be fast.

TECHNICAL SPECS

ENGINE	65-degree V-4 cylinder, 4-stroke, liquid-cooled, double overhead camshafts, four valves per cylinder
DISPLACEMENT	999.6cc
TORQUE	86 ft-lbs (117 Nm)
WHEELBASE	55.9 in (1420 mm)
GEARBOX/DRIVE	6-speed, chain-drive
POWER	181 bhp
TOP SPEED	180 mph (290 kph)

The RSV4 is compact, fast and looks good on the track.

This bike is said to have cost around 25 million Euros to develop. Aprilia's aim was to create not just a bike that was competitive in its group, but the best superbike in the world. That meant going head-to-head with long-established bikes such as the Honda Fireblade, Suzuki's R1 and the equivalent models from the other factories such as Ducati and Kawasaki. With the RSV4 the manufacturers certainly achieved their goal. The mechanical and electrical elements provide a performance to match any of the competitors' four-cylinder engined bikes. That said, it still has the great characteristics of an Aprilia. The look of the bike, which was styled by Migual Gazzuzzi, more than indicates its determination to be recognised.

This bike always looks, sounds and rides as well as any of the oppositions' offerings, if not better. With great performance, great rideablility, distinctive headlight arrangement and plenty of engine and frame on show, this bike is a fantastic result for Aprilia's efforts.

Aprilia also added a celebratory machine to recognise the bike's success, which looked magnificent in Max Biaggi's colour scheme. Whichever model you ride, this bike is monstrously fast – all models are capable of 180 mph (290 kph). It gives the rider bags of confidence in corners, has superb ride quality and looks great.

This bike may have cost 25 million Euros to develop, but it was worth it.

HONDA CBR1000 RR FIREBLADE

This bike is a benchmark, it's the class leader, or one of an elite few at the very least. The 'blade' as it is known has been around since 2004 in its current form. It is the successor to earlier RR models. CBR900 RR was the first model way back in 1992. Sporting a 999cc engine, this bike is capable of some serious acceleration that matches any of the competition and it will achieve a top speed of 180 mph (290 kph). It is a superbike in every sense of the word.

This bike has its roots in racing. Updated versions of the CBR1000 RR Fireblade have been made virtually every year since its introduction. In 2005, Honda equipped the 'blade' with a compact, liquid-cooled inline four-cylinder engine and a cassette-type six-speed gearbox. They gave it a new ram-air system, dual-stage fuel injection, and a host of electronics, such as computer-controlled butterfly valves. More recently the bike received a new 999cc engine which did not hit the red-line until 13,000 rpm. It gained a new cylinder block, titanium valves and ABS braking – the Fireblade was the first production superbike to be fitted with ABS.

The bike continues to race in many different arenas. John McGuiness rode this bike when he won the Isle of Man TT races, and Jonathan Rea rode a Fireblade in the World Superbikes Championship. It's a real winner for Honda both on the track and on the road.

Accessing the 178 bph on this bike comes with ease – no dramas, just pure unadulterated power. From a standing start over 0.25 miles (0.4 km), this bike will reach 150 mph (241 kph)! The ABS system is computer controlled, meaning that when the brake is applied the bike sheds speed smoothly, with no sensation of the pulsing action within the caliper. So, not only does this motorcycle go fast, its stopping and cornering are also excellent. The CBR1000 RR Fireblade gives the rider confidence through acceleration, sheer speed, stopping and cornering. It says to the competition, "Here I am, this is what I can do. Beat that."

Top: The Honda CBR1000RR Fireblade. With its roots in racing, and great to ride as a road bike, this is a class-leading vehicle.

Right: The Fireblade, being put through its paces by a test rider.

TECHNICAL SPECS

ENGINE	liquid-cooled, inline 4-cylinder
DISPLACEMENT	999cc
TORQUE	83 ft-lbs (113 Nm) @8500 rpm
WHEELBASE	55.4 in (1410 mm)
GEARBOX/DRIVE	6-speed, close-ratio, chain-drive
POWER	178 bhp
TOP SPEED	180 mph (290 kph)

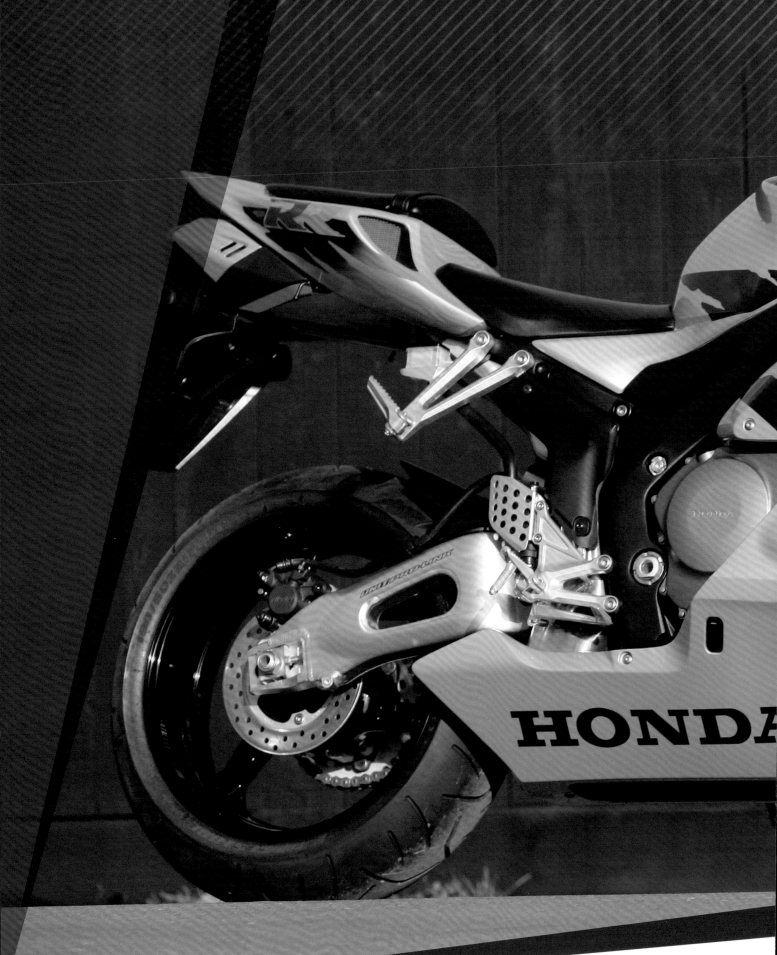

The Fireblade, capable of great speed a result of the 999cc, inline, 4-cylinder engine.

The XZ 10R, pictured above in distinctive Kawasaki green, will give the rider everything they want; speed and mid-corner stability.

KAWASAKI ZX 10R

This bike is a missile on two wheels. It is unbelievably, even obscenely quick. The bike hits the "agreed" maximum speed for production motorcycles of 186 mph (299 kph) with blistering acceleration and good handling ability. The bike is not for those of a nervous disposition. With the four-cylinder, 16-valve engine mounted in an aluminium frame and a close-ratio gearbox, the ZX 10R really is a proper superbike.

Introduced in 2004, the ZX 10R is the Japanese manufacturer's latest offering to the superbike category. It is a class-defining bike. Its engine revs like a supersport 600, it takes flight as though it is trying to catch Captain Kirk's Enterprise and reaches 186 mph (299 kph)! This should not come as any surprise as the bike has been developed, like many in the superbike category, using technology from race bikes.

Top: The Kawasaki in the green livery earnt the bike its nickname "the lean, mean, green machine".

Bottom: This bike shouts 'speed' with its sharp angles.

TECHNICAL SPECS

ENGINE	4-stroke, liquid-cooled, double overhead camshafts, four valves per cylinder, inline-four
DISPLACEMENT	998cc
TORQUE	83 ft-lbs (113 Nm)
WHEELBASE	56.1 in (1425 mm)
GEARBOX/DRIVE	6-speed, chain-drive
POWER	197 bhp
TOP SPEED	184.34 mph (296.6 kph)

Over the years the handling abilities of the Kawasaki ZX 10R have
improved and it is happier on bumpy roads than the early models.
It is quick and effortless to turn, stable mid-corner, letting the rider
change lines with conviction. The inline, four-stroke engine has
grunt. It has a massive amount of torque with 185 bhp. The ZX 10R
has benefited from race bike developments and for a production
superbike it is bristling with race-developed technology. The rider
can select a 'power mode' allowing a choice of power delivery
styles and power levels. The latest versions have Sport-Kawasaki
Traction Control (S-KTRC). This system is designed to monitor
wheel speed, throttle position, engine rpm and other data to ensure
the maximum amount of traction. To push the ZX 10R to its limits as
a rider, you need to know what you are doing and it is probably best
done on a track, not the road. That's where the rider will experience
the intense exhilaration of riding this incredible superbike.

The thrill of riding knee-down with the help of the ZX10R.

FAST MOTORBIKES
180-200 MPH

The Ducati 1199 Panigale seen at the Bangkok International
Motorcycle Show. Exquisite.

DUCATI 1199 PANIGALE

The 1199 Panigale is captivating in every way. The looks are sleek and irresistible, the engine is sublime and the unmistakable Ducati soundtrack is the cherry on the top of a beautiful Italian cake. Open the throttle with enthusiasm and this big twin doesn't shy away from the task. It kicks with gut-wrenching power from the 1198cc, L-twin with four desmodromic valves per cylinder. This is a proper rider's bike.

The naming of this bike breaks with Ducati tradition. By adding a name to its stated engine capacity, it gives the bike an association with Ducati's roots in the Borgo Panigale area of Bologna, Italy, Ducati's birthplace.

Top: The powerhouse of the Panigale.

Middle: It might not be Ducati red, but the Panigale still looks good in white.

Bottom: Designed to flow the oncoming air over the rider. At top-speed, the rider shelters behind this bubble.

TECHNICAL SPECS

ENGINE	superquadro, liquid-cooled, 90-degree L-twin, 4 valves per cylinder, Desmodromic
DISPLACEMENT	1199cc
TORQUE	98.1 ft-lbs (133 Nm) @9000 rpm
WHEELBASE	56.6 in (1437 mm)
GEARBOX/DRIVE	6-speed, wet multi-plate slipper clutch, chain-drive
POWER	195 bhp
TOP SPEED	180 mph (290 kph)

The Panigale is brimming with technology to give the rider the ultimate superbike experience. It contains Ducati's Traction Control system (DTC) and this new iteration is much smoother than earlier versions. To get through the gears it is fitted with Ducati's Quick Shift (DQS) which gives a smooth delivery of power to the rear wheel. The Panigale R's chassis is a monocoque aluminium frame, the engine is the new 'superquadro' L-twin and the bike makes use of the latest electronic rider aids to control the power. It produces a claimed 195 bhp, which means that it has a tremendous power to weight ratio. The 1199 Panigale R delivers smoothly through the power curve reaching its top speed of 180 mph (290 kph) in lightning quick time. Stopping this bike in a smooth and controlled way is achieved with the aid of Ducati's Engine Brake Control system. The bike has Öhlin suspension front and rear and selectable power delivery modes, which means that this bike is a proper, stable Ducati in fast corners.

Is this Ducati's best superbike ever? It has everything. Track derived electronic magic, breathtaking acceleration and blistering top speed and…it has the looks. This bike will definitely apply the 'grin factor' to any rider's face.

It is clear to see why the Panigale is one of
the most sought-after high-speed bikes.

YAMAHA YZF R1

You don't talk about the 'Yamaha YZF R1' – it is such an icon it is simply known as the 'R1'. A sensational sports bike with a 998cc inline four-cylinder engine with an ultra-short stoke, a cross-plane crankshaft and irregular firing intervals. That comes direct from MotoGP and Valentino Rossi's YZR-M1!

The engine is a little shy of 180 bhp and in the latest models, is housed in a Deltabox aluminium chassis, which results in great cornering. With this frame/engine marriage, the bike fires out of corners as good as, or better than, any of its classmates from other factories. The acceleration is absolutely outstanding and it achieves 185 mph (298 kph) when it's flat out. Earlier R1s produced in the mid-2000s were a little slower, only hitting a top speed of 182 mph (293 kph).

The bike has been available since 1998 when it was fitted with a 998cc, liquid-cooled, 20-valve, double overhead camshafts, inline four-cylinder engine which had 150 bhp. This early version of what is now a much-loved bike was capable of nearly 170 mph (274 kph). In later models, from around 2007, it had a 16-valve arrangement producing just short of 180 bhp and could achieve speeds of 185 mph (298 kph).

TECHNICAL SPECS

ENGINE	16-valve, inline 4-cylinder, liquid-cooled
DISPLACEMENT	998cc
TORQUE	85 ft-lbs (115 Nm)
WHEELBASE	55.7 in (1415 mm)
GEARBOX/DRIVE	constant mesh, 6-speed, chain-drive
POWER	179 bhp
TOP SPEED	185 mph (298 kph)

Top: The Yamaha R1 at rest.

Middle: The R1, pictured here in blue, boasts a 998cc engine that is capable of reaching 185 mph (298 kph).

Bottom: The R1, bathed in sunlight and looking every inch the bike it is.

Open roads and an R1. On sunny days, what more could you wish for?

The Yamaha YZF R1 benefits, like other Yamaha models, from being fitted with Yamaha Chip Control intake and throttle systems. More recently it has gained a six-stage traction control system, including anti-wheelie which were both developed for racing. This bike has won races in the British Superbike Championship and World Superbike Championship and the MotoGP M1 model needs no introduction to its pedigree. The R1 is of course toned down a *little* for the roads. Even so, it delivers acceleration, speed and exhilarating power extremely effectively. The bike's competition from Kawasaki, Aprilia and others all have their unique selling points but the R1 is probably the best of the bunch when it comes to a road bike.

There must be a big smile behind that visor!

Sports tourer's with big 1199cc engines can also be fun.

The ZX-12R fairings provide a comfortable touring experience.

KAWASAKI NINJA ZX-12R

The ZX-12R is a sports tourer but it also capable of attention-grabbing performance. For example, accelerating 0–100 mph (0–161 kph) in fewer than 5 seconds! Not bad for a bike that is roomy, has a touring riding position and will keep on pulling your arms off until it hits 185 mph (298 kph).

Production of the Kawasaki ZX-12R began in 2000 and ended in 2006. It was at the time, Kawasaki's contender for the title of fastest production motorcycle. When it was introduced the ZX-12R was a competitor to Honda's Blackbird and the Suzuki Hayabusa. This bike was Kawasaki's premier sport bike. The bike has a claimed 178 bhp from the 1199cc transverse four-cylinder engine which, like any big capacity machine, will deliver its power from very low revs in any of its six gears. The bike was developed over the years with changes including a strengthened crankshaft, some clever engine tuning, new bodywork, radial brakes and fuel injection modifications to name few. Interestingly, in 2002 this bike was not available in the distinctive Kawasaki green colour scheme! The green was back in 2003.

TECHNICAL SPECS

ENGINE	16-valve, transverse 4-cylinder
DISPLACEMENT	1199cc
TORQUE	98 ft-lbs (133 Nm) @7500 rpm
WHEELBASE	57.1 in (1450 mm)
GEARBOX/DRIVE	6-speed, chain-drive
POWER	178 bhp
TOP SPEED	185 mph (298 kph)

For a sports tourer the Kawasaki handles well, not just in the corners but at slow speeds in traffic. This bike is, of course, happy cruising and with good wind protection ensuring the rider is comfortable even at high speeds, and without flattening themselves on the tank to "get behind the bubble". The ZX-12R was never as popular as the Blackbird from Honda or the Suzuki Hayabusa, which is difficult to fathom. It did appeal to many riders as it has all the right characteristics – speed, handling and build quality.

Owners of the Kawasaki ZX-12R are more than happy to sing its praises. This bike has character, in a good way. Designed to be an able tourer the only downside of such a bike is that it might feel a little restricted and stifled when navigating town centres. Apart from that it is great at what it does – and does so over many miles. The engine is more than happy doing high mileage, the rider is happy in a comfortable position with plenty of enjoyment to be had. However, with no grab rail for the pillion, they must hang on when the rider decides to speed up.

The ZX-12R was discontinued in 2006 and replaced by the Kawasaki ZZR1400, but in its six years of production this bike gave the competition a very good run for their money.

The look of a sports bike, yet with superbly comfortable seats. A great-looking bike.

The 'Gixer thou' in the recognisable blue and white colours of Suzuki.

SUZUKI GSXR 1000

The GSXR 1000 was introduced in 2001 to replace the GSX-R1100. It is powered by a liquid-cooled, 999cc inline four-cylinder, four-stroke engine. This bike immediately went for top spot in the big bike league. The inaugural "Gixer-thou", as it became referred to, was hitting 180 mph (290 kph) and thrilling riders with massive power on tap. Through the years of development, Suzuki made it lighter, smaller, easier to handle and faster. It is one of a group of bikes whose top speed is limited to 186 mph (299 kph) for road use.

The Suzuki GSX-R1000 has always had a fantastic engine and is an accomplished road bike. It is also happy getting stuck into fast track day activities. It is up there with the best of the bunch. It's engine is a 999cc, four-stroke, four-cylinder, liquid-cooled, with double overhead camshafts. This is housed in Suzuki's aluminium twin-spar frame and is fitted with big piston Showa front forks (one of the first bikes to do so) resulting very nimble steering. Right from the start this bike was a hardcore sports bike with speed and decent handling, and compared to others of the day, it wasn't too uncomfortable either. Suzuki used gel seats, designed a good riding position and fitted fairing that allowed air to flow over and around the rider.

Top: The GSXR 1000, compact and business-like.

Middle: The Suzuki's fairing and headlight arrangement.

Bottom: Jules Cluzel, making the most of his GSXR 1000.

TECHNICAL SPECS

ENGINE	4-stroke, 4-cylinder, liquid-cooled, double overhead camshaft
DISPLACEMENT	999cc
TORQUE	86 ft-lbs (117 Nm) @10,000 rpm
WHEELBASE	55.3 in (1405 mm)
GEARBOX/DRIVE	constant mesh, 6-speed, chain-drive
POWER	182 bhp
TOP SPEED	186 mph (299 kph)

As the GSXR 1000 has always been exceptional, how do you improve it? Suzuki have improved some of the bike's weaker points, such as the handling, by giving it a lighter feel. The bike now has more mid-range power and better brakes. It also has the Suzuki Drive Mode Selector (S-DMS). This is an electronic rider aid system which allows the rider to select one of three fuel injection and ignition system maps, adjusting power delivery to suit the riding conditions or rider's personal preference.

Somewhat surprisingly, this bike is not loaded with race developed technology like some of its competitors. It doesn't have traction control or ABS, making it unsophisticated by modern standards. This may be due to the factory's absence from the MotoGP grid where prototype racing takes place and developments are made. The bike has been raced successfully in other classes such as British Superbike championships and the American Motorcycle Association in the United States.

There is no doubt that the Suzuki GSXR 1000 is a tremendous bike. It is a more than competent offering to the sports bike category, especially on the road.

A great shot of the GSX-R1000 in action, taken from the rear of another bike.

BMW
S1000

There is so much to say about BMW's first foray into superbike production. This bike is one serious piece of engineering and electronic sorcery. It delivers 190 bhp at the back wheel and is packed to the rafters with all the latest race-developed technology. With a top speed of 186 mph (299 kph) and built to a very high standard, the reliability is excellent, as you would expect from BMW. The S1000 hit the streets in 2009 with the RR model and was impressive right from the start.

An inline four-cylinder engine combined with a splendid fuel injection system, good gearbox and gold-medal winning electronics means this bike is definitely aiming to be top of the class. The S1000RR has great speed and handling and tackles everything the rider asks of it, faultlessly. On the initial model, there is a four-option performance mode manual selection system. One of the selectable options is 'rain mode', which reduces the bhp to 150 and smooths the power delivery for wet conditions. Very clever.

It goes without saying that this bike is a powerhouse but because it has traction control, ABS and the afore-mentioned performance selection system, it is also a bike that can be ridden safely at high speeds.

The introduction of the S1000RR Sport model took the first S1000RR, which was already ahead of the competition with it's huge power and cutting-edge electronics, and improved it! The factory did this by introducing a host of small modifications. The result is even smoother power delivery, more responsive steering, better suspension and more refined electronics. Generally, more grunt. BMW even decided the 'rain mode' performance selection should have 163 bhp, up from the original 150 bhp setting, confident that the bike would handle it.

Top: The BMW headlight arrangement using different shapes and sizes.

Right: The BMW S1000, being put through its paces by a test rider.

Further development led to the S1000RR HP4. Compared to a S1000RR, the HP4 weighs 20 lb (9 kg) less, at 439 lb (199 kg), and has a little more horsepower. It has electronic suspension, a 15-stage traction control system and Brembo monobloc front calipers with race developed ABS. It doesn't stop there, this bike also has a quickshifter and electronic Dynamic Damping Control (DDC) on the suspension. It is capable of anything a normal rider can throw at it and it will cope.

TECHNICAL SPECS

ENGINE	water-cooled, 4-stroke, inline 4-cylinder, 4 valves per cylinder
DISPLACEMENT	999cc
TORQUE	82.6 ft-lbs (112 Nm) @9750 rpm
WHEELBASE	56.4 in (1432 mm)
GEARBOX/DRIVE	constant mesh, 6-speed, chain-drive
POWER	193 bhp
TOP SPEED	186 mph (299 kph)

The BMW shows that it has the qualities of a true sportsbike, pictured above.

A rider achieving good lean angles on the MV Agusta F4.

MV AGUSTA F4 1000

The MV Agusta logo looks as though it is from a bygone era of bikes such as the AJS, Matchless and BSA. This motorcycle is light-years ahead of those classics. The F4 1000 is most definitely of its time though. First introduced in 1998, the F4 was created by famous motorcycle designer Massimo Tamburini following his work on the Ducati 916. Although the shape might not have changed much since then, the new models are bristling with a bag full of technology.

The F4 1000 R was the second mass-produced F4 from the Italian factory, following on from the first mass-produced F4, the 'S' model. There was also at the time the F4 1000R CRC Gold limited edition. Both came along in 2006 and were packed with horsepower – 174 bhp in the R and 175 bhp in the limited edition CRC. In August of the same year, an F4 1000 R was used to set the record for the fastest production class 1000cc motorcycle and reached 185.882 mph (299.148 kph) at Bonneville Salt Flats, Utah, in the United States.

The bike was developed further and MV introduced the F4 1000 312 model. It is so called at it was claimed it would achieve a breathtaking 193 mph (312 kph).

Top: The distinctive underseat exhaust pipe arrangement and rear light cluster on the F4.

Middle: The rear of the MV Agusta, showing its 5-spoke rear wheel, chain and sprocket arrangement.

Bottom: Close-up view of the rear of the engine and the exhaust system.

TECHNICAL SPECS

ENGINE	liquid-cooled, inline 4-cylinder
DISPLACEMENT	998cc
TORQUE	84 ft-lbs (114 Nm) @10,000 rpm
WHEELBASE	56. 3 in (1430 mm)
GEARBOX/DRIVE	6-speed, close-ratio, chain-drive
POWER	201 bhp
TOP SPEED	186 mph (299 kph)

The inline four-cylinder engine is powerful and refined. It is claimed that recent F4 R models produce 201 bhp at the crank. They have eight traction control settings, Öhlin suspension, Brembo monobloc brakes and they rev all the way up to 13,700 rpm.

Compared to a Japanese superbike, which tend to give a relatively soft and reasonably comfortable ride, the F4 can feel somewhat less roomy, even cramped. Add to that, the stiffer suspension on the F4 means that doing lots of miles can be punishing on the joints, especially if you are tall.

This bike has speed, delightful styling, an impressive build quality and an exhaust note that brings a smile to your face. Is the MV Agusta F4 R a superbike success? Oh yes, it is stunning.

Even at rest, this bike has the look of a fast machine.

KAWASAKI ZZR1400

I ntroduced in 2006 as the successor to the ZX-12R, the Kawasaki ZZR1400 was billed as the fastest-accelerating motorcycle in the world. A motorcycle that is a big sports tourer and promises lots of speed, this bike doesn't disappoint. Limited to 186 mph (299 kph), the latest models reach these speeds with a gear to spare. It is thought, if it was unlimited and there was a suitable place to test it, this bike would hit 200 mph (322 kph) no problem. That is fast! It's a race bike top-speed from a sports tourer.

The ZZR1400 is fast but it is also a very capable touring machine when carrying a full load, and a good commuter bike too. The original versions had a 1352cc engine which was just as quick as later modified models. This is due to the agreed (by all manufacturers) maximum top speed of 186 mph (299 kph), so that's what it had as a top speed – 186 mph. The ZZR1400 is an insanely powerful bike. Kawasaki claimed the early models had a new generation of engines which were completely different to the ZZ-Rs of the past. The result is a bike that challenges on every level in the big tourer category.

Top: The large front mudguard of the ZZR1400.

Bottom: Large sports tourer yes, but still able to perform sportsbike tricks.

TECHNICAL SPECS

ENGINE	liquid-cooled, 4-stroke, double overhead camshafts, forward-inclined parallel 4-cylinder, 16-valve
DISPLACEMENT	599cc
TORQUE	119 ft-lbs (162.5 Nm) @10,500 rpm
WHEELBASE	54.1 in (1375 mm)
GEARBOX/DRIVE	constant mesh, 6-speed, chain-drive
POWER	133 bhp
TOP SPEED	186 mph (299 kph)

This shot of the bike cornering shows off the four-into-one exhaust underneath the ZZR1400.

Current models have so much more – a liquid-cooled, inline four-cylinder engine with double overhead camshafts and increased capacity. The engine is now 1441cc and has a claimed 207 bhp which takes the rider to the 186 mph (299 kph) mark with one of the bike's six gears in reserve! The ZZR also has Kawasaki's Traction Control (KTRC), three adjustable power modes, a stiffer monocoque aluminium frame and a longer swinging arm. What Kawasaki have produced is a rocket ship on two wheels. All that power is not in any way uncontrollable though. It may not look sexy but it's a sports tourer with a job to do. The Kawasaki ZZR doesn't just do the job. This bike is top dog.

All the upgrades, modifications and styling changes result in a durable sports tourer. Powerful and fast with mind-blowing acceleration but comfortable to ride and with smooth, reassured handling capabilities. What more could you want from a sports tourer? Nothing.

This bike is a great tourer. It's fast, yet comfortable.

FAST MOTORBIKES
RACE BIKES

Spanish rider Marc Marquez rides his Honda during a MotoGP free
practice round of the Argentina Grand Prix. He displays the huge
lean angles that can be achieved 60 degrees from the vertical!

HONDA
RACING

Packing a 1000cc engine, the Honda factory team continue to be a force to be reckoned with in MotoGP. The RC213V, developed from the previous year's 800cc RC212V, is an amazing race and championship-winning bike. Like others in its class, it is lightning quick, full of technology and has a 90-degree V-four, liquid-cooled, four-stroke engine. Also in the MotoGP field are riders using the Honda RCV1000R operated by privateer teams, a bike that is a capable of top-10 finishes despite not having the very latest parts or engine management systems. The full factory spec bike produces 230 bhp. Keeping all of that power on the track is a tricky business and electronic aids are vital. When the bike is cornering at an angle of more than 55 degrees, the last thing a rider wants is for the back wheel to spin and not drive. Traction control systems therefore kick in as the rider opens the throttle.

However, it's not just clever electronics that make this bike such an effective race machine. Engineers developed the RC213V to have a centralised mass, which optimises handling and agility, and maximises grip when cornering.

Top: Dani Pedrosa of Spain and Repsol Honda Team rounds the bend during the MotoGP of Qatar Qualifying at Losail Circuit on March 22, 2014, in Doha, Qatar.

Bottom: Dani Pedrosa of Spain and Repsol Honda Team celebrate taking second place at the end of the MotoGP race during the MotoGP of Argentina. The race took place on April 27, 2014, in Rio Hondo, Argentina.

TECHNICAL SPECS: RC213V

ENGINE	4-stroke, 4-cylinder, liquid-cooled, double overhead camshaft, 4 valves per cylinder
DISPLACEMENT	1000cc
TORQUE	undisclosed
WHEELBASE	56.5 in (1435 mm)
GEARBOX/DRIVE	undisclosed
POWER	230 bhp
TOP SPEED	undisclosed

Redesigns have made the bike lighter and have reduced friction between contacting surfaces. The body work is not just carbon fibre but it's lightweight carbon fibre. Holding it all together is a twin-span aluminium frame, which provides the required balance between stiffness and flexibility. This enables the bike to transfer the engine's power to the back wheel and give the rider some "feedback" as to how the bike is performing.

Honda's bikes are raced in many championships by teams such as Padgett's Race Team in British Superbikes and Honda TT Legends in the Suzuki eight-hour endurance race. They are also successful on road circuits such as the Isle of Man where they have been ridden to success by TT heroes such as John McGuiness. Different modifications and restrictions apply in each ft but one thing remains – Honda continue to be a force to be reckoned with.

Leon Haslam of Great Britain and the Pata Honda World Superbike
in race 2, during round one of the 2014 World Superbike Championship at
Phillip Island Grand Prix Circuit on February 23, 2014, on Phillip Island, Australia.

YAMAHA RACING

The most iconic racing machine from the Japanese factory is the famous Yamaha YZF-M1. This bike is raced in the MotoGP by the factory team and by satellite teams. It is not hard to see why. This successful bike has a 1000cc, liquid-cooled, inline four-cylinder engine with a cross plane crankshaft. Piloted by one of the the world's greatest riders Valentino Rossi, the YZF-M1 has won many world championships. It continued to do so even when Rossi rode for Ducati for two seasons. The bike produces 240 bhp and a top speed of well over 200 mph (322 kph). It has incredible braking ability thanks to the Brembo calipers which have four pistons on each of the two front discs. The bike uses an aluminium twin-tube delta box frame with adjustable steering geometry which enables the bike to turn into corners superbly. It has Yamaha's versions of all the latest electronics, such as anti-wheelie, traction control and fly by wire throttle. Engine map choices allow the rider to choose the most appropriate fuel consumption/power combination at any moment during the race. MotoGP rules limit the amount of fuel that a competing bike can have on board, which means that the rider might need to forego speed in order to finish the race.

Top: A mechanic prepares Jorge Lorenzo's Yamaha YZF-M1 on the eve of the MotoGP of the Argentina Grand Prix at Termas de Rio Hondo circuit, in Santiago del Estero, Argentina, on April 24, 2014.

Bottom: Bradley Smith of Great Britain and Monster Yamaha Tech 3 rounds the bend during the qualifying practice during the MotoGP of Argentina. April 26, 2014, in Rio Hondo, Argentina.

TECHNICAL SPECS: YZR-M1

ENGINE	liquid-cooled, inline 4-cylinder with crossplane crankshaft
DISPLACEMENT	1000cc
TORQUE	undisclosed
WHEELBASE	undisclosed
GEARBOX/DRIVE	6-speed cassette (with alternate gear ratios available), chain-drive
POWER	240 bhp
TOP SPEED	undisclosed

The Doctor at work. Valentino Rossi of Italy and Movistar Yamaha MotoGP lifts his front wheel during the MotoGP of Argentina. Free practice on April 25, 2014, in Rio Hondo, Argentina.

Jorge Lorenzo of Spain and Movistar Yamaha MotoGP heads down a
straight during the MotoGP Red Bull Grand Prix of The Americas race.
April 13, 2014, in Austin, Texas.

In the World Superbike Championship, the Yamaha R1 is the bike run by the Yamaha World Superbike team. The team, previously known as the Yamaha Motor Italia WSB team, was based near the Monza circuit in Italy, and other than a five-year absence (2000–2005), it has been competing since 1995. In 2009, the team won the championship with rider Ben Spies. The Yamaha R1 is not just used by the manufacturer's team, there are many others who also choose the bike, such as Milwaukee Yamaha. They race the R1 in the British Superbike Championship and have had success in road racing. They won the Macau GP in 2009, a very different street circuit surrounded by Armco crash barriers and walls.

In the World SuperSport Championship, several teams run the Yamaha R6 as it is always a very competitive bike in this class. Whichever championship you look at, on a world stage or locally, you will see successful Yamahas competing at the front end of the pack.

Cal Crutchlow of Great Britain and Ducati team rounds
the bend during the MotoGP of Qatar Qualifying at Losail
Circuit on March 22, 2014, in Doha, Qatar.

DUCATI RACING

The Ducati Desmosedici GP is produced to race in the MotoGP Championship. The bike is light at only 353 lb (160 kg) dry, and has a 1000cc, liquid-cooled, 90-degree V-four, four-stroke, demodromic double overhead camshaft engine with four valves per cylinder. This bike is the pinnacle of race bike development and produces 235 bhp, a top speed of 205 mph (330 kph) and that distinctive Ducati exhaust note. The bike is brimming with technology to aid the rider such as traction control, launch control, anti-wheelie, seamless transmission and an electronic throttle system. The list goes on. All of this is housed in an aluminium frame with Brembo brakes and Öhlin suspension – it is a fantastic motorcycle. Ducati have won the ultimate championship but continuous development means boundaries are being always being pushed. Change isn't always easy to package. Ducati have had challenges to overcome as rules change and other teams produce more effective packages. The fight to be the best continues.

Andrea Dovizioso of Italy and Ducati Team lifts his front wheel during the MotoGG of Qatar. Free practice at Losail Circuit on March 21, 2014, in Doha, Qatar.

TECHNICAL SPECS: GP14

ENGINE	liquid-cooled, 90-degree V-4, 4-stroke, Desmodromic double overhead camshaft, 4 valves per cylinder
DISPLACEMENT	1000cc
TORQUE	undisclosed
WHEELBASE	undisclosed
GEARBOX/DRIVE	Ducati seamless transmission, chain-drive
POWER	235 bhp
TOP SPEED	in excess of 205 mph (330 kph)

In the World Superbike Championship the weapon of choice is the 1199 Panigale. This bike has an engine capacity of 1198cc in V-four formation, a six-speed gearbox (not seamless transmission as fitted in the MotoGP bike). There is less technology to aid the rider, as per the championship rules, however, this bike is still capable of speeds of more than 193 mph (311 kph). The World Superbike Championship limits how much money is spent on a racing motorcycle and limits the number of engines a team can use. Why? To make the championship more competitive and available to more teams. As a competitor, Ducati must limit the number of internal modifications to the standard 'off the shelf' Panigale, including changes to the engine.

In the British Superbike Championship, teams again use the 1199 Panigale. The racing version is derived from the standard production Panigale with a limited number of changes. Some of the permissible modifications include modified camshafts and increased rev limits of 750 rpm over the standard bike rpm. Internal engine changes include the fitment of aftermarket connecting rods, however pistons and valves must remain unchanged. These restrictions make it possible for many privateer teams to race, which is great for the sport.

Italian rider Michele Pirro rides his Ducati during the MotoGP free practice of the Argentina Grand Prix at the Termas de Rio Hondo circuit, in Santiago del Estero, Argentina, on April 25, 2014.

Randy De Puniet of France and Suzuki Test Team starts from the pit lane during the MotoGP tests in Sepang. Preparation for the team's return to MotoGP in 2015 on February 26, 2014, in Kuala Lumpur, Malaysia.

Top: Randy De Puniet of France and Suzuki Test Team heads down a straight during the MotoGP Tests in Sepang. Day One at Sepang Circuit on February 4, 2014, in Kuala Lumpur, Malaysia.

Bottom: Alex Lowes of Great Britain and Voltcom Crescent Suzuki in race 2, during round one of the 2014 World Superbike Championship at Phillip Island Grand Prix Circuit on February 23, 2014, on Phillip Island, Australia.

SUZUKI RACING

In the 1970s and 1980s, Suzuki raced 500cc two-stroke machines and Barry Sheene was the superstar of the day. Suzuki are still a big player in motorcycle racing and are currently involved in the World Superbike Championship. They last raced in the MotoGP in the 2011 season and are planning a return in 2015. Suzuki are testing and developing their prototype machine with the help of former World 500cc GP champion Kevin Schwantz and recent MotoGP racer Randy de Puniet. It will be good to see them back in the ultimate racing championship.

The Voltcom Crescent Suzuki Team race in the World Superbike Championship on the GSX-R1000. The bike produces 220 bhp from a Yoshimura-tuned 998.6cc, four-stroke, four-cylinder, liquid-cooled, double overhead camshaft, 16-valve engine. The factory estimates the bike's top speed at just over 200 mph (322 kph), making it very competitive indeed.

In the AMA Pro SuperBike Championship in the United States, the Yoshimura Suzuki Racing Team are also vying for success with the GSX-R1000

Suzuki bikes are also involved in national championships. In 2013, Suzuki's bikes won both the New Zealand Superbike and Supersport championships. It is not just the GSX-R1000 that is winning, in the Supersport class it was the GSX-R600 machine that achieved the top spot.

TECHNICAL SPECS: GSX-R1000

ENGINE	Yoshimura tuned 4-stroke, 4-cylinder, liquid-cooled double overhead camshaft, 4 valves per cylinder
DISPLACEMENT	998.6cc
TORQUE	undisclosed
WHEELBASE	undisclosed
GEARBOX/DRIVE	constant mesh, 6-speed, chain-drive
POWER	more than 220 bhp
TOP SPEED	estimated 202 mph (325 kph)

On the roads, the Tyco Suzuki team are winning with road-racing heroes like Guy Martin. They complete in many events such as B'ol d'Or, Ulster Grand Prix, the Isle of Man TT, Oliver's Mount Scarborough and Northwest 200. These are all very different to purpose-built race circuits but the bikes are achieving great results in the UK.

The GSX-R1000 has also demonstrated it's endurance racing capabilities by winning the Suzuka eight-hour race in both 2007 and 2009, breaking Honda's domination of the event. The team use three riders over the eight-hour period. Interestingly, the Suzuka circuit, or the Suzuka International Racing Course to give it its full title, was originally designed as a Honda test track in 1962 and has a 'figure 8' layout, of which there are very few in the world.

So whatever championship, whatever bike, Suzuki are competitive and winning races at both national and international levels. Long may it continue.

Eugene Laverty of Ireland and Voltcom Crescent Suzuki during Superpole, ahead of round one of the 2014 World Superbike Championship at Phillip Island Grand Prix Circuit on February 22, 2014, on Phillip Island, Australia.

APRILIA RACING

In 2004, Aprilia become part of the Piaggio Group, who specialise in racing bikes. Although Aprilia are not currently in the MotoGP with 1000cc bikes, they have been very successful in the 125cc and 250cc races. However, the big-engined Aprilia is racing well at a world level in the World Superbike Championship. The factory team first entered the championship in 2009 with the Aprilia RSV4 1000 Factory. The race machine is allowed to have some changes made to it under the World Superbike Championship rules. The track version of the RSV4 1000 Factory is fitted with an Aprilia Racing engine control unit (ECU) to manage the ignition and fuel injection for increased performance. It also has the latest generation electronic throttle, traction control and anti-wheelie systems.

Using the V-four longitudinal double overhead camshaft, 999cc engine, this bike has been extremely successful – it is a championship-winning machine.

In its first season racing in the World Superbike Championship, its rider Max Biaggi won one race and was placed nine times. The following season this bike went on to greater things with Biaggi winning the championship. He stayed with Aprilia, ending his career in 2012 by winning the championship for a second time for the Italian factory on the RSV4.

In the United States, the RSV4 1000 Factory is raced in the AMA Pro SuperSport series. Interestingly however, in order to compete, the bike has to be modified so that riders can only turn the throttle half open. This series is for 600cc engine bikes but the organisers wanted to add more manufacturers. Therefore to enable more bikes to take part they allowed larger capacity machines, such as the RSV4 1000, to compete. As the large machines were quicker, they had to be slowed down and a compromise to 'level the playing field' was agreed. Any team racing a large engine bike had to restrict the throttle.

Roll on the return of Aprilia to the premier MotoGP class. It will make for exciting racing if their World Superbike success is anything to go by.

Davide Giugliano of Italy riding the #34 Althea Racing Team Aprilia during the World Superbikes Race One at Phillip Island Grand Prix Circuit on February 24, 2013, on Phillip Island, Australia.

TECHNICAL SPECS: RSV4 SBK

ENGINE	liquid-cooled, double overhead camshaft, 65-degree V-4, 4 valves per cylinder
DISPLACEMENT	999cc
TORQUE	undisclosed
WHEELBASE	undisclosed
GEARBOX/DRIVE	6-speed cassette gearbox, chain-drive
POWER	226 bhp
TOP SPEED	undisclosed

Sylvain Guintoli of France and Aprilia racing team, helped on his way down the pit lane during round four of 2013 Superbike FIM World Championship at Autodromo di Monza on May 11, 2013, in Monza, Italy.

Sylvain Guintoli of France and Aprilia Racing Team in race 2, during round one of the 2014 World Superbike Championship at Phillip Island Grand Prix Circuit on February 23, 2014, on Phillip Island, Australia.

Colin Edwards rides his Kawasaki during a free practice session
ahead of the Italian MotoGP at Mugello's circuit on May 31, 2013.

KAWASAKI RACING

Kawasaki have been winning races for more than 45 years in many classes and many championships. In 2003, the Kawasaki Racing team was formed and at that time raced the 990cc ZZ-RR. Their current bike of choice is the Ninja ZX-10R. The Japanese manufacturer has been extremely successful in the AMA SuperBike Championship, winning it nine times. In 2009, they suspended their involvement in MotoGP but continued to be compete in the World SuperSport and World Superbike series. By constantly improving the impressive ZX-10R, Kawasaki have ensured that this competitive bike has evolved into a winning bike. So much so that the ZX-10R won the prestigious World Superbike Championship in 2013.

There are two types of bike used in the World Superbike Championship: the Ninja ZX-10R and the Evo bike. The Evo bike (which is also based on the ZX-10R) is aimed at complying with a second set of rules which describe more restricted modfications allowed to a bike. The aim is to reduce costs and make it cheaper to race competitively in the championship. In 2015, the Evo rules for modifications will apply to all bikes racing in the World Superbike Championship. Until then both classifications of superbike will race in the same race at the same time. However until 2015, the Evo bikes will be slightly less competitive.

Top: Sheridan Morais of South Africa and Iron Brain Kawasaki SBK during practice ahead of round one of the 2014 World Superbike Championship at Phillip Island Grand Prix Circuit on February 21, 2014, on Phillip Island, Australia.

Bottom: Patrick Jacobsen of the United States and Kawasaki Intermoto Ponyexpres during round one of the 2014 World Supersport Championship at Phillip Island Grand Prix Circuit on February 23, 2014, on Phillip Island, Australia.

TECHNICAL SPECS: ZX-10R

ENGINE	4-stroke, liquid-cooled, double overhead camshaft, 4 valves per cylinder, inline-4
DISPLACEMENT	998cc
TORQUE	undisclosed
WHEELBASE	undisclosed
GEARBOX/DRIVE	6-speed, chain-drive
POWER	undisclosed
TOP SPEED	undisclosed

In the Evo class, each team has a limit of eight engines per season and a limited number of gear ratios. There is also a cap on the cost of suspension and brakes. Privateer teams can also be competitive in this new class – the rules state that they can buy a bike from the manufacturer at a fixed price. Therefore, privateer teams and manufacturer teams have the same starting point. The privateer teams will also receive updates and maintenance from the manufacturers during the season.

Evo bikes are very fast. On race track straights they have achieved speeds in excess of 175 mph (282 kph). As these bikes have basically the same engine as the road bike it is inspiring to observe them in the hands of professional riders. For those riders and spectators who appreciate the efforts of the engineers, mechanics and riders it is a joy to see the Kawasaki 'lean, mean, green machine' performing to the limit and winning.

Loris Baz of France and Kawasaki Racing Team during practice ahead of round one of the 2014 World Superbike Championship at Phillip Island Grand Prix Circuit on February 21, 2014, on Phillip Island, Australia.

FAST MOTORBIKES
SPECIALISED BIKES

DODGE
TOMAHAWK

The Dodge Tomahawk is most definitely a concept bike. It looks as though it has been graphically generated for a fictional Hollywood superhero. However, it is not an animation, it is real, street-legal concept bike. It was exhibited in 2003 at the North American International Auto show in Michigan, Detroit, although only nine were ever sold to the public.

Initially, Dodge claimed that the bike would achieve a top speed of 420 mph (676 kph), although this was later revised to 300 mph (483 kph). This has never been proven. In fact it is believed that the bike has never been ridden above a speed of 100 mph (161 kph). There are some people who believe that the bike would require a lot of streamlining and the addition of fairings in order to stop the rider being ripped off the top of the bike.

When it was first exhibited, Dodge said that they would demonstrate the bike's capabilities at the Bonneville Salt Flats (the venue for world-record speed attempts). So far this has not taken place.

The engine is a 90-degree V10 which has a staggering 8300cc capacity and produces 525 ft lb (712 Nm) of torque and 500 bhp! It has only two gears but two front wheels and two rear wheels configured side by side, initially giving the appearance of a single wheel front and back. These wheels move independently, to help steer around corners.

As for the rideability, cornering and comfort of the Dodge Tomahawk, should we really care? It's a concept bike, and concept bike design is all about pushing the boundaries. The designer, Mark Walters, is to be congratulated, he really did do just that with this bike.

The Dodge Tomahawk, shown at the North American International Auto Show.

TECHNICAL SPECS

ENGINE	Chrysler 90-degree V10 (designed for use in the Viper sports car)
DISPLACEMENT	8300cc
TORQUE	undisclosed
WHEELBASE	undisclosed
GEARBOX/DRIVE	2-speed
POWER	525 ft-lb (712 Nm)
TOP SPEED	claimed 420 mph (676 kph)

The concept bike, showing the two independent front wheels and a hint of the huge engine.

V4

A bike with a helicopter gas turbine engine needs
a substantial exhaust system, as shown.

MTT
Y2K

Marine Turbine Technologies (MTT) is located in southern Louisiana, United States, and is run by Ted McIntyre II, the CEO and president. MTT delivers custom, diverse turbine installations for many applications. The MTT Turbine Superbike, known as the Y2K Turbine Superbike, is one of them. This is no ordinary bike. It contains a Rolls Royce Allison Model 250 gas turbine engine, which is normally used to power helicopters and small aircraft. Previously, bikes have used aircraft jet engines but the MTT design team, headed by Chritian Travet, took a different approach. They used the Rolls Royce turboshaft engine, a two-speed gearbox, and chain and sprocket to drive the rear wheel, enabling this beast to hit 227 mph (356 kph).

The Y2K is a street-legal bike and was the first turbine-powered bike in the world. It produces 320 bhp and 425 ft lb (576 Nm) of torque. The engine is housed in a tubular steel frame, which also holds the bike's transmission fluids and a reserve fuel tank. Although not light by any stretch of the imagination, it is fitted with carbon fibre fairings and even has a rear facing camera. You wouldn't want to get too close to anything while parking – the exhaust kicks out a lot of heat.

According to its riders, the Y2K has the ability to scare beyond belief and whilst its creation is an exercise in flexing engineering knowhow, there is no real place for it in the market. The cost of this bike is immense and only a few are able to afford one. Perhaps it was never meant to be anything other than what it is, a fete of incredible engineering.

TECHNICAL SPECS

ENGINE	Rolls Royce Allison 250 series gas turbine
DISPLACEMENT	undisclosed
TORQUE	approximately 425 ft-lb (576 Nm) @2000 rpm
WHEELBASE	68 in (1727 mm)
GEARBOX/DRIVE	2-speed automatic
POWER	more than 320 bhp
TOP SPEED	estimated 227 mph (365 kph)

The current world record holder in its cigar-shaped streamliner, which houses a twin Suzuki Hayabusa engine.

TOP OIL
ACK ATTACK
STREAMLINER

Currently the fastest motorcycle in the world is the Top Oil Ack Attack Streamliner. Mike Akatiff, the owner and founder of Ack Technologies, designed the bike. It is a fully streamlined motorcycle that encloses the rider in a cylindrical cockpit.

Way back in 1907, the world record for the fastest motorbike was 136.27 mph (219.31 kph) and this record stood for an amazing 20 years. In 1956, the first modern, fully streamlined motorcycle record was set at 214 mph (344 kph) by the Texas Cigar. This was around the time that record attempts were starting to take place at the Bonneville Salt Flats in Utah, United States, and they still are today. Speeds are calculated as an average of a two-way run. The Top Oil Ack Attack is a bike that is specifically designed and constructed with one thing in mind – holding the record for its classification. The record this bike set in September 2010, when piloted by Rocky Robinson, was 376.363 mph (605.714 kph). Now, that is fast!

It has a Chomoly tube, bullet shaped chassis housing twin Suzuki Hayabusa engines, each with a capacity of 1299cc. The calculated horsepower exceeds 1000 bhp and it runs on two piece aluminium wheels with tyres designed to run at speeds more than 500 mph (804 kph). This massive power needs a specialised engine management system to enable the team to collect data about the machine's performance, and to ensure safety as much as is possible. After the bike achieves these speeds, it must be stopped. This is accomplished by deploying two parachutes. One is used to slow the bike from speeds above 330 mph (531 kph) and the other is an emergency chute that is hopefully never needed.

Not satisfied with setting the current record, the team are attempting to build a bike that will achieve more than 400 mph (644 kph) on average. Only time will tell if they can achieve their goal.

TECHNICAL SPECS

ENGINE	dual Suzuki Hayabusa engines with turbo charger
DISPLACEMENT	2598cc
TORQUE	undisclosed
WHEELBASE	144 in (3658 mm)
GEARBOX/DRIVE	6-speed gearbox for each engine
POWER	1000 bhp
TOP SPEED	376.363 mph (605.714 kph)

MISSION RS

Mission Motorcycles is an American company based in San Francisco, California, founded in 2007 by Forrest North and Edward West. The company's aim is to create high-performance, electric motorcycles, and that is exactly what they have done with the Mission One, Mission R and the Mission RS. These are fast bikes.

The Mission One, designed by Yves Béhar, has a top speed of 150 mph (241 kph), which is not bad for an electric bike. It was entered into the Isle of Man TT Zero race in 2009 where it finished fourth with an average speed of 74.091 mph (119.238 kph) over the 37.75 mile (60.75 km) mountain circuit. In the same year this bike won the AMA electric motorcycle land speed record at the BUB Motorcycle Speed Trials held at the Bonneville Salt Flats. The bike achieved a 150.059 mph (241.497 kph) average over a two-way run.

The Mission R uses technology and engineering knowledge gained and developed for the Mission RS. The Mission RS is a limited edition bike and only 40 were produced. Both bikes have 120 kW (160 bhp) electric motors providing 120 ft lb (163 Nm) of torque to power them. The torque is not dependent on engine revs as it doesn't have an engine, so is available as soon as the throttle is twisted.

These machines are devoid of the moving mechanical parts of conventional bikes – no pistons, crankshaft, or clutch rotating thousands of times per minute. This means a riding experience unique to electric bikes, especially when cornering. The bikes provide linear power delivery using what Mission call the InfiniteDrive™ powertrain. Hence no need for a gearbox or clutch.

The rider also has an instrument cluster that supports integrated GPS, bluetooth, ride telemetry and navigation display. The screen is high resolution and touch sensitive. As electric bikes continue to develop, other electronic devices and rider aids will be become more common as standard fittings. The Mission bikes certainly prove that electric bikes can be fast as well as being "green".

Top: Electrical components of the Lightning in detail.

Right: The electric bike looks great and can also hit a top speed of 150 mph (241 kph).

If electric bikes are the future then Mission, and a few other manufacturers, are leading the revolution and showing us what is possible. They demonstrate to the adrenaline-driven, speed-loving motorcycle fans that electric bikes, although silent, can achieve speeds high enough to maybe one day convert them from the petrol engine bike they know and love.

TECHNICAL SPECS

ELECTRIC MOTOR	liquid-cooled 3-phase AC induction with 120 kW output
DRIVE	Mission motorcycles Infinitedrive™
TORQUE	120 ft-lb (163 Nm) from zero revs
TOP SPEED	150 mph (241 kph)

The Lightning, seen here competing at
Pikes Peak in Colorado, United States.

LIGHTNING
SUPERBIKE

Since Lightning's formation in 2006 by Richard Hatfield, the Lightning organisation has been driving forward the technology of electric vehicles, including motorbikes. The team's efforts have been rewarded with land speed records in 2009, when it achieved 166.388 mph (267.776 kph) setting the new record, and in 2011 when it achieved a top speed of 218.637 mph (351.862 kph) and a combined average of 215.96 mph (347 55 kph) in Utah, United States, at the Bonneville Salt Flats. The bike has also achieved other firsts throughout its development. In 2006, it was the first Electric Sport Bike with more than 60 bhp and a little short of 70 ft lb (96 Nm) of torque, enabling a top speed of 100 mph (161 kph). It may have been an early prototype but it already demonstrated the shape of things to come. In 2010, the bike was the first Zero Emission North American Road Racing champion and in 2011 it was the first electric bike to break 200 mph (322 kph).

The bike is not just fast, it is successful in competition too. In 2013, Carlin Dunne rode a Lightning Motorcycles electric bike to beat conventional motorcycles at Pikes Peak in Colorado, United States, posting a time of 10 minutes 00.694 seconds over the 12.42 mile (19.98 km) course. The bikes have also had success on the race tracks too, such as at the FIM EPower Championship at Le Mans in France, and they have also had wins in the Isle of Man TT zero emission class.

The bike is propelled by a liquid-cooled 125 kW+ motor which runs at 10,000 rpm and has a 370V, 12 kWh battery pack. The bike is capable of completing 150 miles (241 km) on a fully charged battery pack, if ridden sensibly. At motorway speeds the battery pack lasts about 100 miles (161 km).

Electric bikes are not a new idea. The first patent was filed for an electrically powered bike in the late 19th century. It was of course a far cry from today's incarnations of electric bikes. However, as Lightning and others drive the technology forward and race organisers provide them with the opportunity to show off what is possible through prototypes, it would appear that this could be the way forward for motorcycle development, especially in a world ever more conscious of the effects of using fossil fuels. For the traditionalists amongst us, let's hope they develop a way of giving us the appropriate sound track to go with fast motorbikes.

Below: While driven by an electric motor, the Lightning benefits from traditionally-shaped aerodynamic fairings.

TECHNICAL SPECS

ELECTRIC MOTOR	liquid-cooled with 125 kW output
BATTERY PACK	370 V 12 kWh
TOP SPEED	215.960 mph (347.554 kph)

Racing and winning the FIM Epower race in Laguna Seca, United States.

STREETFIGHTERS

A streetfighter! What is it? It's the result of an individual's efforts to customise a fast bike, usually giving it a more aggressive, unique look and a different sound. There are many fantastic examples out there created by talented people with an eye for styling a bike to make it stand out from the crowd.

Usually, but not always, these bikes start life as a standard big-engined superbike with the usual paint job. Take one of these bike, be it a Honda Fireblade, Suzuki Gixer Thou, Yamaha R1 or any of the other manufacturers top superbikes, and take the fairings off, and it immediately looks different. A lot of streetfighter bikes are fitted with twin, round headlights, reminiscent of the 1960s café racer. Add more upright handle bars, change the exhaust system to a shorter and of course louder one, and you are on your way to completing your streetfighter. There are a huge variety of parts now available on the market for those wishing to change the appearance of their bike and turn it into a more individual machine – brake levels and clutch levers of different colours, shapes and sizes, foot pegs, hoses, instrument clusters to name but a few. In later years, custom-build frames have been designed, ordered and built and elaborate paint designs have been applied to produce beautifully crafted bikes.

Although this style originated "on the street", eventually the factories recognised that if they produced bikes in this style there would be a market for them. So, we now have factory produced bikes such as the Ducati Streetfighter, which actually uses the name in the model. In some ways this sort of defeats the object of a streetfighter – individuality.

There are, thankfully, lots of magnificent examples of streetfighters. Original, personal and housing those superbly fast engines that make every rider, spectator and interested observer smile every time they see or hear one.

Top: Without fairings, this streetfighter's exquisite frame and engine are visible, plus it has a simple but effective colour scheme.

Right: A great-looking streetfighter. Customised with gold and red livery, straight handlebars, gold engine covers and a single headlight.

TECHNICAL SPECS

Streeetfighters are customised versions of any bike the owner chooses. That bike could be from any manufacturer and be any model, therefore technical specs will vary from bike to bike.

The Ducati 848 and Husquvana Nuda, typifying the streetfighter look.